F

THE ART OF

MW01031883

Joanne Sawicki, creator, Channel Health TV: "I know Ed and Deb [Shapiro] as their television producer, and they walk their talk."

Bernie Siegel, MD, best-selling author, *Love, Medicine and Miracles*: "Ed and Deb Shapiro are two warm, caring, and capable individuals. Their work makes our planet a safer and more loving place to live."

Sharon Salzberg, author, *Lovingkindness* and *Real Love*: "Ed Shapiro shows us that deep, mindful relaxation is an art we can all master. By sharing the wisdom of yoga nidra practice, he gives us the keys to live with greater joy and peace of mind. *The Art of Mindful Relaxation* invites us to reshape how we relate to everyday situations and attain a greater sense of ease."

Stephen Levine, international best-selling author: "I hope that your work is reaching many. It deserves it, and so do they."

Seane Corn, cofounder, Off the Mat, Into the World: "Ed Shapiro's informative and inspired book should be on every yoga practitioner's shelf! I have used yoga nidra since I first began yoga and can vouch for its brilliant effectiveness. Transformation is not possible without first being deeply relaxed, and this book provides the skills that can help get you there. Highly recommended!"

Ram Dass, author, *Be Here Now* and *Still Here*: "Ed and Deb [Shapiro] bring compassion and heart to a modern world where it is sorely needed."

Gangaji, American spiritual teacher: "Ed and Deb Shapiro are long-term leaders in the international spiritual community. Ed's new book demonstrates the weight behind that leadership. With intelligence and great humor, he reveals what appears to be hidden to, in fact, be obvious. His writing supports the reader in directly discovering what too often feels out of reach—the wonder of true peace. I wholeheartedly recommend this book."

Rep. Tim Ryan (D-OH): "Change is inevitable and can be transformative in positive ways, but if we put it off, then we put living on hold, fixed in old ways of being. Ed Shapiro's new book shows us how to have the courage to embrace change. This is a necessary and timely book."

Cyndi Lee, author, *May I Be Happy*: "I've never read a book like this before! The wisdom of mindful yoga nidra goes far beyond telling us that chilling out is good. Ed Shapiro guides us through profound dynamic relaxation, helping us uncover layers of who we think we are, while giving us the rich practices that help us live into who we want to be, through the mindful, loving practice of truly becoming familiar with ourselves. This is intelligent, spiritual self-care for the whole world."

Kitaro, Golden Globe– and Grammy Award–winning musician: "Ed and Deb [Shapiro] make a connection to their friends' spirit. They then bring their spiritual energy all over the world for world peace."

Judith Ansara, teacher, coach, author, *The Bones We Once Belonged To*: "Ed Shapiro is a wise guide, gently reminding us how to live a mindful and peaceful life, no matter what our circumstances. If you embrace the practices he offers, I have no doubt you will find yourself happily on the path he has already traveled."

Andy Puddicombe, cofounder, Headspace: "There are many teachers of meditation, but there are few who can so effortlessly translate such profound and ancient techniques. An authentic, accessible, and enjoyable guide to relaxation."

Chloe Goodchild, singer, spiritual teacher, author, *The Naked Voice*: "This book reveals the essential components of perennial wisdom in an accessible form that enables you to live safely, courageously, and compassionately. Ed Shapiro is a multifaceted, modern-day mystic with a wild sense of humor, who has dedicated his life in service to humanity. He invites you to relax, remember, and live in the NOW, with the skills to unify breath, body, heart, mind, and soul. These are transformative teachings of a rare contemporary spiritual teacher."

Lord Andrew Stone of Blackheath, United Kingdom: "In understandable language, this book gives us the theory and knowledge of mindfulness, why we need to practice, and the compassionate and loving benefits that ensue. I have been practicing mindfulness for many years, yet here I found new knowledge, greater compassion for myself, and learned to deepen my awareness."

Deva Premal and *Miten,* musicians, recording artists: "There is a special music that arises from the sound of silence. Ed Shapiro invites us into this sacred dimension, which is so essential in the midst of this very busy world."

Mark Matousek, author, *Sex Death Enlightenment* and *Writing To Awaken*: "As a prolific author, ordained swami, and spiritual provocateur, Ed Shapiro has spent the past thirty years carving out a place for himself among mindfulness teachers that's both dogma-free and refreshingly unique. If you're interested in reducing stress, increasing your joy, and deepening wisdom in your life, buy this book!"

Jonathan and Andi Goldman, authors, sound healers: "Just the act of reading this magnificent book creates deep relaxation and mindfulness. Applying the information and exercises within it brings even more centering and inner peace. What a blessing!"

Margo King and *John Steiner,* transpartisan and sacred activists: "Ed Shapiro shows us how to deeply relax and be at peace, so we don't squander the immense gift of our life. Then we can awaken to our true self!"

Christine Stevens, author, *Music Medicine*: "Modern-day-meditation author Ed Shapiro shows us the art of relaxation, the space between the notes, in this masterpiece from ancient India to daily life."

Dr. Lex Hixon: "The wonderful Shapiros are a conduit of joy and spiritual energy that heals hearts on their subtle level."

THE ART OF MINDFUL RELAXATION

THE HEART OF YOGA NIDRA

ED SHAPIRO

EDITED BY DEB SHAPIRO

ixia
PRESS

MINEOLA, NEW YORK

Bibliographical Note

The Art of Mindful Relaxation is a new work, first published by Ixia Press in 2018.

International Standard Book Number

ISBN-13: 978-0-486-82441-3
ISBN-10: 0-486-82441-1

Ixia Press
An imprint of Dover Publications, Inc.

Manufactured in the United States by LSC Communications
82441101   2018
www.doverpublications.com/ixiapress

Dedicated to the Truth within all beings

CONTENTS

ACKNOWLEDGMENTS

I am deeply grateful to my wife, Deb, who has helped beyond words; I couldn't have done this without her. Thanks to our editors, Fiona Hallowell, Stephanie Castillo Samoy and Nora Rawn, who have been there every step of the way, and to Bill Gladstone, my great agent. To Jimmy, Jane and Splash Cronin; Megan, Rob and Dakoda Larson. To Ruth and Ken Leiner, Mort Shapiro, Parmita Pushman, Anne Bancroft, Julie Carpenter, Andy and Mary Dinsmoor, Margo King and John Steiner, Elvira Bernier, and Raji and Rani. A special thank you to the magical Johnny Fox and to all my teachers, both past and present.

PART 1

MINDFUL RELAXATION

SEEKING PEACE

Ever wonder what the biggest problem in life really is? Yes, it's stress! And the remedy? Profound dynamic relaxation. This is a true story: I met John at a stress-release workshop I was teaching in Scotland. He was a schoolteacher in a run-down area of Glasgow. As if that wasn't hard enough, he was a history teacher, a subject that most of his pupils were completely uninterested in—perhaps the history of rap music but certainly not of kings and queens! Teaching had become a source of immense stress; John would regularly lose his temper and was planning to quit. I saw him again a year later at a follow-up workshop. John looked refreshed and radiant, so I fully expected to hear that he'd gotten a different job. Instead, he told me that he'd become head of the department. The difference? John had done nothing other than Yoga Nidra, the relaxation practice this book teaches you, and he did it every morning before going to school. This had led to a state of deep acceptance and mindful relaxation. As a result, both his attitude and approach at work had radically improved. Being mindfully relaxed is the ultimate life-changing gift we can give ourselves.

Ever since the beginning of time we have encountered stressful situations, starting with cavemen who had to hunt for food and the resulting fight-or-flight dilemma when confronted with wild animals. The stress-producing factors may be different now but they have the same effect. It's quite amazing to me that after thousands of years we still haven't figured out how to relax!

Unless we can look at stressful difficulties with mindful awareness then all we really do is create more stress; a tense mind creates greater tension, while a calm and clear mind creates clarity and positivity. When we are stressed everything becomes an irritation, no matter how well intended. Friendships are lost and families broken as achievements and possessions become more important than kindness and caring.

We can't hide from stress, but we often take being stressed for granted without doing anything about it until it becomes unmanageable. We know what we have to do, but believe that relaxation can be accomplished by indulging in mindless and distracting activities. At times this is true. But more often it's an escape from our inability to cope in a world of conflicting ideas, pressures and prejudices. As the anxiety becomes too much to handle we begin to look outside ourselves for help, such as to alcohol, drugs, or therapy.

Stress throws us into regrets of the past and fears of the future and so we lose the ability to be in the present moment. Meanwhile, guilt, shame and blame create unimaginable scenarios, as the ego-mind is constantly preoccupied with itself. Such is our "normal" state of being!

You may need to ask yourself: Do I get upset or angry when matters don't go as planned? Do I need to be in control, or can I allow events to take their natural course? Do I always think I am right and that others must be wrong? Am I able to see things as they are without prejudice or bias? Do I bear grudges and hold on to things or can I let go and move on? These are important issues to look at honestly in order to become more tolerant, kind and easeful.

Confusion and misunderstanding make us desperate for change, but we don't know how to bring about the transformation we yearn for. So we change the superficial things, like our hairstyle or clothes. We may even have a facelift or hair transplant. All we want is to be wanted! But if we change our lives from within then our outer self will also transform.

Being at ease has a hugely positive effect on our looks, health, on others, and the world we live in. What more could we want?

The Workings of the Mind

We are surprisingly ignorant about our mind, this brilliant instrument of ours, and have a very limited idea of how to delve deeper to discover its true depth and magnitude. We go to professionals to fix us, or we take prescribed drugs to calm us down. But instead of turning to external "cures," we can get to know the variations of our psyche; just as we care for our body we can learn to care for our mind, to keep it clear, creative and peaceful.

A stressed mind buries itself in chaos and confusion. We react to simple issues as if they were matters of life and death, we vacillate trying to make a decision, and easily get angry or upset over small incidents. The mind is like the flame on a candle that can't exist without wax to burn; it's always searching for fuel to power its thoughts by reaching outward for satisfaction through the senses, which act like magnets, attracting and distracting at every opportunity.

Due to the mind's tendency to be scattered and unable to focus we don't know how to trust ourselves. Ever notice how mental chatter can go on endlessly, flitting from one subject to another, as we get lost in memories, create fantasies or act out dramas? Most of us take it for granted that this is the way it is: this is just who I am! We overanalyze and immerse ourselves in insecurities, doubts and fears.

As our energies disperse we get run-down and depressed, so stress easily becomes distress. Feeling overwhelmed, we avoid, deny, hope it will go away, or become distracted by mindless activities like partying, watching too much TV or binge eating. We get absorbed with anything that helps us sidestep our problems, anything that will even temporarily divert our attention.

Sitting in an easy chair with our feet up has become synonymous with being relaxed, as has saving up all year for a vacation. Running away from our problems seems like a good solution but we rarely get the true rest or relaxation we long for. We are in a hurry, racing through life, getting nervous and irritated; rushing to work, rushing to eat and rushing to sleep, we wonder why we get so tense. So then we rush to go on vacation in order to relax!

But wherever we go and whatever we do, there we are, along with all our conflicts, stresses, irritation, mood changes and depression lurking behind our every action. A selfish mind causes tension, is unstable and unaware. Beneath it we really do want true happiness, but we get lost in our attempts at finding it. We can be in prison behind bars and be free, but we can walk freely in the world and be enslaved.

When life is going along smoothly it's easy to smile, but if someone hurts or abuses us, can we still feel okay? Constantly confronted with situations that bring up frustration, irritation or anger, we long to overcome our limitations, but then we get triggered again and want to shout or even hit someone. Except that if we hurt someone we ultimately hurt ourselves, as such negativity will affect us physically, emotionally and mentally. If we can really grasp the consequences of negativity we will grow in greater awareness.

The mind and body are our instruments, our vehicles for moving from one state of awareness to another. It's possible to experience extraordinary levels of consciousness when we expand the mind and are enriched by the vast wealth available within us. As the great American jurist Oliver Wendell Holmes said, "Man's mind, stretched to a new idea, never goes back to its original dimension."

Relaxation and Mindfulness

Relaxation is relatively simple, yet it is highly misunderstood; we think: "If I do this or that I will relax and then I will be better." But our relaxation will stay both superficial and temporary if we don't bring mindful awareness to it. Mindfulness means paying attention to something, focusing awareness on it, and awakening that awareness in our whole being. When we are mindfully relaxed we are consciously aware of letting go on a deeper, long-lasting and profound level.

The practice of relaxation I teach is Yoga Nidra, which comes from the ancient yoga sutras. The long-lasting effect of Yoga Nidra is a mindful relaxation that permeates our lives, influencing our every thought, word and action. Mindfulness enables us to let go of repetition and compulsiveness. We begin to respond confidently rather than mindlessly reacting, develop more positive attitudes and make clearer choices. Circumstances are neither good nor bad; it is our response that makes them either positive or negative. Change the response and we change our world.

Nothing in life is permanent; the thoughts, desires and beliefs we had yesterday may not even pertain to today, regardless of how much energy we put into them. We try to solidify everything, to hold on and make our existence secure, yet at any moment the rug can be pulled out from under us, and everything changes. No matter who we are, life is temporary; there are no guarantees, no real security. Indecisiveness and wanting things to be different from how they are inevitably cause greater confusion. We make plans, but they always change. I often ponder John Lennon's words from "Beautiful Boy (Darling Boy)": "Life is what happens to you while you're busy making other plans."

But all is not lost! Life need not be a hopeless mess, nor do we have to be at the mercy of our thoughts. It is possible to change our way of being. We just have to find out how to use the keys that unlock the vast treasures within. Mindful relaxation clears out the storehouse of negative past impressions embedded deep inside, creating a fresh new slate; it is an attitude, a state of mind, and a way of being. It is the key to greater awareness. Think of the stressed mind like a mirror that has accumulated much dust. We have to clean and polish this mirror, for only then can we see our true reflection.

2

THE JOURNEY

Many of us have gone on some sort of quest looking for answers to our questions, problems or the meaning of life, maybe travelling to the East to seek guidance, to the South to meet shamans, or going to numerous seminars and workshops. It was during my own journey to India that I first discovered Yoga Nidra and recognized its far-reaching effects.

I grew up in the Bronx in the 1950s. It was a tough time; always there was a sense of frustration and fear in my neighborhood, of being troubled. It was unfriendly, even antisocial. But by the late 1960s I'd moved into Manhattan and noticed a change with a new energy growing, a consciousness-expanding change. It was the era of the hippies and became known as the "love generation."

At first, a group of friends and I created a communal lifestyle in the heart of New York City. We became vegetarian, took LSD, read esoteric books, and studied Zen meditation and Buddhism. We read Alan Watts, Ralph Waldo Emerson and Henry David Thoreau, the philosophers and transcendentalists. These inspired us to delve deeper and find more of their meaning. But we were also looking for a teacher, someone who was a living example of all that the books were saying.

I was changing. I felt love everywhere, an inner joy was always with me, leading to profound experiences. Yet it all seemed so contrary to the life I grew up in that it was hard to know what was real and what was my imagination. Here I was, a kid from the streets of the Bronx. I grew up avoiding street fights, going to high school dances, even winning New York City dance championships, hanging out at Studio 54, and now I was getting a spiritual calling?

I was told about a holy man who had come to Manhattan from India. He was a Swami who taught yoga and apparently radiated joy, unconditional love and peace wherever he went. At that time, the idea that happiness could be found by relaxing and quieting the mind was unheard of, or that we could individually experience deep peace or bliss. This was too esoteric, too mystical. It was more common to think that having a good time meant going to a faraway island, partying at a fancy hotel or watching a cool movie! In fact in those days a Swami was usually depicted looking into a crystal ball, and a yogi would have his legs wrapped around his neck in contorted positions.

We went to see this Swami. He had long hair and a long beard, and he wore saffron-colored robes. It was an extraordinary moment. True teachers emanate peace, tranquility, loving-kindness, warmth and bliss; they are magnetic and you feel drawn to them from deep within. This Swami was the first teacher I'd ever met, and definitely the first person I had ever encountered who radiated such qualities.

I began to understand that the state I was witnessing in the Swami was pure egolessness; his very existence was for others, which he expressed in all his actions and teachings. That first meeting was enough to show me that divine qualities could be realized within. In particular, he taught that leading an unselfish life is the most rewarding path to follow, as desire (for accolades, for wealth) is an endless chain that never ends and can only bring pain. To lead a selfless life, however, can bring deep joy and insurmountable happiness.

We started attending yoga classes, learning hatha yoga and pranayama (postures and breathing exercises), purifying our bodies and cleansing our minds. I began spending more and more time engaged in my practice, determined to make my life a reflection of higher ideals, of meaning and service.

It was then that I met another Swami who was visiting New York City from India. Still a novice, I was unsure what to expect. After a welcoming dinner I was asked to escort this second Swami to his car. As I walked with him he seemed very different from the Swami I was used to: the first was tall and graceful, gentle and sensitive in his manner, while this one was short and solid, precise and blunt. He told me that the other Swami was like a loving father, but he himself was a military captain. That statement, along with the time I spent with him, sparked a longing to train with him. So when I was invited to India to stay at this Swami's ashram (a spiritual community), I was ready to go.

It was 1968. People all over the United States were going through radical changes. I knew Tim Leary, Allen Ginsberg, Richard Alpert (who is now known as Ram Dass) and other contemporaries who were influencing the consciousness of so many, but I wanted to find out for myself the root of what was going on within me. So when folks began heading West to San Francisco with "flowers in their hair," I headed East.

While living at the ashram in India I was taught Yoga Nidra. What this ultimately showed me was that unless we are truly relaxed we can't progress; our forward motion is handicapped by our inability to go within and ease the inner stresses we all have. All of our past is registered deep in our minds, determining our motivations and actions. To release these blocked energies we need to relax enough so we can explore the boundlessness beyond the content of the mind.

True Change Comes from Within

How we react to stresses and tensions is the root of most of our personal problems, as they throw us off-balance and we become less able to function fully. There are over seven billion people living together on this planet and we all influence each other, even if we are unaware of it. We can communicate anywhere and everywhere instantly, yet simultaneously there is deep misunderstanding that keeps us feeling mistrustful and in a state of confusion and fear of each other.

Having made great advances in science and technology, we are still primitively slow in understanding ourselves and there has been little progress in unfolding the vast realms of the unconscious mind. While we have been happily conquering outer space we have discovered very little about inner space! Yet, we are all here together, experiencing the same difficulties. No one is higher or lower than another, no matter what one's position or status in life. The king, president, beggar and thief are all part of the same reality.

I felt this most strongly when my wife Deb and I met the Dalai Lama in India. Deb went to touch his feet in the traditional manner but he made her stand, saying, "We are all equal here." Yes, we all breathe the same air and walk the same earth; and if a rich man and a poor man were both held under water, I guarantee that their only thoughts would be for breath, not for riches or wealth.

Unfortunately, we often lose sight of this. Most of us carry guilt, shame, anger and fear around with us like a sack of antiques filled with issues from the past and worries about the future. This leads us to becoming self-centered and uncaring about what happens to others as long as we are all right. In the process we lose touch with the basic qualities of giving and compassion, dominated by our fear of being without. The pain we feel in ourselves we then blame on others; we are at war with each other just as we are at war within ourselves. So how can we be at peace in this world if we are not at peace at home?

What we can do is let go of how we think things should be and stop blaming others or the world for how we are, stop blaming ourselves for being incompetent when we fail or make mistakes, and stop putting ourselves down for being stressed and thinking we will always be this way. We can change!

Why Are We Here?

Here we all are on a beautiful planet, revolving in space. It's a wonder, it's awesome; to call it anything less than a miracle would diminish its grandeur. Deep within each of us is a tremendous richness we can contact during those times when we are quiet and peaceful. However, within this greatness we may feel very insignificant and see life as having no real purpose or meaning. The perennial question "Why are we here?" is one we usually prefer to avoid. The wise ones tell us it is to awaken and realize the truth within, but for many of us this is just too vast, incomprehensible, and the question seems unanswerable.

Invariably the confusions and stresses we deal with become compounded, and as these traumas accumulate in our unconscious they crowd out those quiet times of reflection and we lose touch with our deeper purpose or direction. Whatever affects us personally also affects every one of us, even though the ego persists in believing we are separate from each other. We have to break through this illusion to find our peace.

Just as a lotus flower grows from a mound of mud, emerging with a pristine flower, so we have dense mud in our minds that hides the budding flower within. Mental limitations, negative views, fears, repressions, doubts and confusions form the foundation of this mud. But just as the lotus needs the mud from which to grow, so this mud is the very nourishment we can use to develop, expand and realize our true nature. It is the fertile ground from which our inner lotus can bloom.

We really are capable of moving from a state of stress to one of relaxation. There is a way through the mire to the green fields beyond. Others have been here and have left directions, signposts for us to follow. It's the most important journey we can take in this life.

3

WHY WE NEED TO RELAX

I was discussing stress at a mindfulness retreat when Joe, an attendee, shared how he didn't get stressed over any one thing because everything is stressful to him and he wakes up already stressed. Sound familiar?

We have all experienced stress and its close companion, anxiety. In small doses stress is somewhat beneficial as it can heighten awareness, but in big doses on a daily basis it begins to have a very debilitating effect. At least two-thirds of doctor visits are due to stress-related symptoms, while absenteeism and lost productivity costs businesses approximately three hundred billion dollars a year. Stress and anxiety are major contributors, either directly or indirectly, to six of the leading causes of death in the United States, namely coronary heart disease, cancer, lung ailments, accidental injuries, cirrhosis of the liver, and suicide. The three best-selling prescription medications are for anxiety, hypertension and ulcers, all stress-related symptoms.

Stress weaves its way into every area of our lives. Frustration, insecurity, fear, guilt, and depression are the most common factors that turn stress into distress. We have explored and exhausted so many areas of life, but we have yet to learn how to relax within ourselves. This is especially a problem considering there are no medications that will change our circumstances, get us a new job or see us through a divorce. Rather we must find our own ways to cope. Watching television or going on vacation rarely has a long-lasting effect; it's more like putting a Band-Aid on a broken leg. So more enduring relief has to be found within and by ourselves.

The Biochemical Effects of Stress in the Body

Are you restless, irritable, forgetful, or feeling overwhelmed? When we first experience stress an alarm is sounded in the brain. The hypothalamus is a small part of the brain in an area known as the limbic system and it's here that the alarm sounds to create the "stress response." The initial stress factor may be as simple as the recollection of a painful memory or too many bills coming at once; but when your brain detects a stressful situation the stress response immediately goes into action by releasing the hormones cortisol and adrenalin.

As stress increases we become unable to adequately adapt, easily overreact to issues, lose a clear perspective on priorities, get muddled or disorganized, become increasingly depressed, or we may rant and rage for no apparent reason. Most important is the feeling of being unable to cope, that events or demands are beyond our control, and therefore failure is looming. We get locked into repetitive self-criticism that only serves to reinforce feelings of hopelessness.

When the stress response continues over a period of time, with a regular release of stress hormones and the resulting physiological and emotional changes, we begin to experience more serious problems. High levels of cortisol can wreak havoc on the brain, causing it to shrink in size and make fewer new brain cells. This sets the stage for depression, and even Alzheimer's disease.

The limbic system is known as the seat of emotions, as it's here that our emotional states and responses are experienced in the brain; this area also monitors many of our bodily functions, thereby linking the emotional effects of stress with physical health. For instance, the hypothalamus regulates the autonomic nervous system, which in turn regulates heart rate, digestion and metabolism, blood pressure, respiration and reproduction. It is, therefore, hardly surprising that when the alarm is sounded it leads to heart problems, excessive sweating, digestive disorders, ulcers, impotence, and so on.

The sympathetic nervous system gets ready to deal with stress through the secretion of particular hormones that prepare us for fight-or-flight action. But when the stress is not actually life threatening, even though our bodies respond to it as such, we have to deal with the excess hormones left in our system. When there is no war to fight or animal to hunt, where do the hormones go? What happens to the body when the stress response is experienced without any means of expression? How does the digestive system cope with being suppressed once, maybe twice a day, or even more often? Is it hard to believe that ulcers or irritable bowel syndrome are connected to high stress levels, that we get constipation, diarrhea, or a loss of appetite? What happens to the urge to scream, to lash out, or find some release from the tension? Is it surprising that marriages suffer, that alcohol and food addiction is rising, or that mental exhaustion leads to breakdowns?

The physical results of excessive stress can include headaches, diarrhea, high blood pressure, grinding teeth, heart palpitations, hyperventilation, disturbed sleep, backache, loss of appetite, asthma, skin rashes, excessive sweating, dry mouth, hives, restlessness, fidgeting, nail-biting, to name but a few. Psychological symptoms may include depression, anger, inappropriate or excessive elation, rapid or dramatic mood changes, anxiety, excessive eating or sudden weight loss, impaired concentration, loss of memory, confusion, irrational fears, indecisiveness, self-consciousness, disorganization, changes in appearance such as sloppy dressing, poor self-care, halting speech, impotence, sexual promiscuity and phobias. That's quite a handful!

The effects of emotional stress are even harder to resolve as we find it so difficult to freely or openly express our feelings. We bottle up our conflicts until they become buried in the unconscious. Mental stresses create a jumble of confusions until we become way too immersed in such chaos to find our way out. The manifestations may include increased anxiety and panic, irritability and frustration, irrational outbursts of anger or hostility, power and manipulation issues, debilitating fear and insecurity, rapid mood changes, restlessness and nervousness, sexual problems such as impotence and frigidity, addictive behavior, memory loss, paranoia and confusion, impaired performance and concentration. Phew!

The hormones that circulate as a result of the alarm signal also have the effect of numbing our feelings to the point where we may not even be aware we are becoming stressed. In the battlefield we would be grateful for such numbness, but in ordinary circumstances this means that we may continue being stressed, if not distressed, yet not experience the debilitating effects until much later, when we collapse, exhausted.

As stress has such a wide-ranging effect on us, it is hard to define which illnesses are stress-related and which are not, but studies confirm that debilitating stress is strongly associated with numerous diseases and ailments. Perhaps it is simpler to say that stress affects every part of our body, mind and emotions, so it's essential that we understand it more deeply and learn how to cope with it.

What Really Is Stress?

Despite the weakening effect on our bodies, stress itself is not really the issue. Rather, it is our reaction to it that determines its effects. In other words, stress is not an independent entity that invades our lives, but rather the result of how we meet our challenges or difficulties. It makes no difference what the stress-producing factor may be; it is the way we react to it that counts, as a potentially stressful circumstance can be stimulating and uplifting if we perceive ourselves as being able to cope, while if we feel overwhelmed or helpless then distress is sure to follow. Dr. Kelly McGonigal's book *The Upside of Stress* covers the related research on this at length; but in short, our framing narratives for our experiences are key to their impact.

So how we deal with a situation determines the effect that it has on us. The body doesn't know the difference between a real threat and an imagined one: a coil of rope in the dark will equally stimulate the stress response as will a real snake. It is our perception that determines our response. And by changing our mind-set we change the perception.

A stressful reaction may also be the result of experiences or repeated modes of behavior that react to situations in a certain way and trigger the inner alarm signal, as in Pavlov's dogs. All our past traumas and experiences are recorded in the unconscious where they make deep impressions, known in yoga as *samskaras*, a Sanskrit word meaning mental impressions that influence us from an unconscious and subconscious level. These impressions constantly influence our conscious mind, determining how we make decisions or why we behave in certain ways. They hold us in fixed patterns, which create the limitations we then need to shift if we are to be stress-free and relaxed.

Language can also be a stressor by creating negative attitudes or reactions. For example, when we consistently repeat words such as terrible, awful, scary, or frightful, we are imposing a pattern in the mind. By repeating them, or other negative words, their associated feelings awaken and they start having a literal effect that can set off the stress alarm. Common phrases that give the mind an impression of fear or of being threatened include "I can't stand it," "It's killing me," or "This is going to be the end of me." It's irrelevant whether the threat actually exists or not, as there's still a rush of adrenalin even when it does not.

Doubt is a big stressor, whether it's doubt in ourselves or doubt that everything will be okay. The smallest amount of doubt that comes into our mind about whether things will go well immediately creates fluctuations that begin to cause chaos and confusion, leading to stress. This opens the way to nervousness and fear: if I don't lock the door someone's going to break in, etc. So stress can be a response to the expectation that negative things will happen, as well as our doubt that we'll be able to deal with them, which is a sort of built-in self-destruction clause.

So depending on how we react to the events in our lives or how we feel we are being treated, tension levels can rise. Especially if we believe we are useless or helpless, as stress will increase or decrease based on how we see the relationship between ourselves and our world.

There is also a misunderstanding, often held by people who tend to live life on the edge—like those involved in sports or in highly competitive businesses—that we have to be stressed or feel like we're walking a tightrope in order to succeed; that the drive for ever greater challenges is needed in order to stimulate creativity and efficiency, and that without it our responses will be too inert or passive.

However, excess stress actually diminishes performance rather than giving it a boost; it may work in the short term but can lead to burnout in the long term. There is a far more effective mind-space where we are both fully relaxed and totally alert at the same time, a state of dynamic relaxation that encourages greater creativity. In a relaxed state we have access to far greater physical and psychological energy levels—which is why stress management is an integral part of most forward-thinking businesses. The greatest lesson we are learning, both individually and collectively, is that we can work with our stress response and develop a higher level of adaptability, resulting in far-reaching positive effects on every aspect of our lives.

Being vs. Doing

In order to reduce the effect of stress we need to be aware of when we are "doing" so much that we forget about simply "being," since a balance of both is essential for our psycho/emotional balance. We are human beings, not human doings! We put so much energy into doing that we lose touch with the ability to just be, to feel our own presence, to appreciate the raindrops on a leaf, to watch the sun go down, or talk with our loved ones. Are you so caught up in activities that you have no time to walk barefoot in damp grass, to dance or sing? How can you bring more balance into your life?

Let's be realistic about our needs and desires, and make our goals appropriate. To aim too high and not get there is only going to cause distress. Rather than seeing the things that happen as hindrances hampering our way, we can turn them into opportunities to grow in patience, tolerance, compassion and creativity. As we relax, we begin to make friends with ourselves, become our own ally, deepen our sense of self-worth, self-esteem, confidence and inner strength.

We can move out of a weak or negative sense of ourselves by developing an awareness of personal power and inner strength. However, it's important to make a distinction here. Personal power is not about having power over someone or something; it doesn't involve manipulation or control, nor is it a self-centered or egotistic state where we are only concerned with our influence over others. Rather, personal power arises out of self-knowledge, out of a bond of friendship and love with ourselves, and beyond that to an awareness of our interconnectedness with all beings. The more deeply we meet ourselves, the greater our sense of self as a part of the whole. Personal power emerges from that place where dignity, inner strength and interconnectedness meet.

4

THE COURAGE TO CHANGE

To develop a relaxed mind it's important to cultivate a supportive lifestyle, which probably means making changes. We tend to be very attached to our habitual way of living, even if it's detrimental to our physical or psycho/emotional health. The old patterns are comfortable and familiar, we are very accustomed to them—this is who I am and I can't help it!—whereas change seems unknown or beyond our capabilities.

Within ourselves we do know where changes are needed, but making them always seems to lie somewhere ahead of us, in some other place or time. How often have you said, "I must exercise more" or "I must stop getting so angry" or "Next week I will start relaxing," but you just keep putting it off, until you never actually do it. Do you feel bound by commitments, work, family or the needs of others? How often has guilt stopped you from taking time for yourself? How often have you longed to scream but instead put on a stoic and capable smile? Does change seem like an impossible dream?

Letting go of the old and familiar may also mean going deeper into ourselves to discover what we truly believe. Our parents and teachers instilled many of our behavior patterns that remain embedded in our unconscious minds. We grow up absorbing their attitudes toward religion, race, sex, money, work, relationships, even the meaning of life, and may not have the emotional distance to see which of our beliefs we have inherited rather than chosen. We are formed by generations that have gone before us, but we don't have to maintain those beliefs if they no longer serve us. It's important to recognize this so we can find what we actually feel for ourselves, even if it means stepping outside the box and shifting the images people have of us.

For example, I grew up in an Orthodox Jewish family in the Bronx that believed Judaism was the only way. I wasn't even allowed to bring non–Jewish friends to play in my house. But through my Yoga Nidra training I was able to release the deep and ingrown attachments to such beliefs and embrace other faiths. I even become a Swami in the yoga tradition!

Change is the essence of life. When we put off change then we put living on hold, staying stuck, entrenched in the past and fixed in old ways. While change may be uncomfortable at first, it can also be transformative; when we have the courage to embrace it then we can embrace life. The same life force that enables a weed to grow through six inches of concrete is within us too, constantly reaching for inner peace and happiness. Rather than blaming our parents for having passed on to us their prejudiced, paranoid or confused views, we can be grateful that we now have the awareness to find our own truths.

Awareness itself is transformative. As we bring awareness to our entrenched psychological and emotional patterns they will lose their grip. Change is possible because inside us we do know there is a free and joyful being, someone who is truly happy, caring and loving. Let change bring fresh possibilities, let us see with new eyes and new awakenings! If we are open to change, it needn't have a stressful impact—it can be a very welcome challenge.

You may want to do the **TIME-OUT** below with someone who can be a "relaxation buddy," such as a friend or partner.

TIME-OUT: *Making Changes*

This exercise helps you see where you are holding on to old ways of being. Become an observer of yourself for at least one week. Keep a daily journal of your feelings, and at the end of each day take a moment to reflect, particularly on those areas where you feel stuck. Observe and note your reactions, attitudes, behavior and resistance.

Do these states actually reflect how you feel or can you see where you are reacting out of old patterns, perhaps in a way that your mother or father did? Make a note of any place where you feel your response did not express the real you.

Now replay the scene and ask yourself how you would do it differently if you were following your own feelings. What would you say? What would you do? Breaking the molds of old patterns may feel a little threatening at first, but can bring a tremendous sense of liberation, as if you are letting go of a great weight or burden.

Self-Delusion and the Ego

Our lives are the means we have to find a deep inner peace and to realize our true nature. Yet they can often feel far too crowded with problems, disappointments and suffering for us to realize such truths. We become too preoccupied with self-survival and self-preservation to reach for a greater meaning beyond ourselves.

In our desire to avoid failure, conflict and distress, it is natural to look for ways to protect ourselves from such predicaments. But in so doing we create a buffer around ourselves, hiding from the world in our familiar comfort zone, rarely allowing anything in that threatens our sense of security. And although we may think we aren't stressed and that everything's really fine, just beneath the surface we find the tension that is seen when we bite our nails, play with our hair, talk or eat compulsively, tap our feet repetitively or pace up and down. This is stress!

The ego is the "me, my and mine," the me-centered mind-set that creates separation, greed and selfishness. We have a compulsive need to serve this self-proclaimed master. Like a dog with a bone, the ego clings to dramas, to the "I'm right and you're wrong" scenario, or to having power over others—and it won't let go. By paying attention to our physical and psycho/emotional reactions we can determine when we are being drawn into a tight or constricted state by the ego, which reacts with stress responses when it feels threatened. Then, after observing these dynamics in ourselves, we can begin to change a stressful response into a stress-free one.

TIME-OUT: *Assessing Personal Stress*

This exercise will enable you to assess your stress to help you determine where change is needed. Sit quietly with some paper and a pen. Answer those questions that are most applicable to you. The purpose is not to judge or blame, but to develop greater self-awareness by recognizing and alleviating the stressors in your life.

About Your Family

Has there been a major change in your household, such as children leaving home, a loss or death?
Has anyone in your family been experiencing a particularly difficult time, such as school exams or job redundancy?
Is anyone ill and in need of your care?
Can you respond differently to family issues?

About Your Relationships

Is a disagreement always your partner's fault or can you see your part in the problem?
Are you able to express your feelings?
If you had the ideal partner, how would it change you?
Can you respond in a different way to your partner?

About Yourself

Do you get irritated or annoyed easily?
Do you dislike yourself?
Are you addicted to anything?
What can you do to encourage and empower yourself?

About Your Health

Do you feel tired or get run-down easily?
Do you get regular exercise?
Do you spend any part of the day being quiet and reflective?
If you felt good about yourself, what would you do differently?

About Your Work

Do you feel unable to do what is being asked of you?
Does your work environment feel depressing? Sad? Loud? Pressured?
Do you feel unfulfilled? Unacknowledged? Unrecognized?
Can you do anything differently at work or in your attitude to it?

Peace Is Within

In a state of true relaxation we discover a deep stillness of body and quietness of mind, a level of peace and harmony that is out of our reach if we are stressed. Discovering deep relaxation is an ongoing process, rather than a one-off event. It involves having the right attitudes and motivation, of recognizing our habits, strong and weak points, and nonjudgmentally accepting them. It means being willing to take time out to go within, as well as being willing to disregard the voice of the ego.

A mind that is truly at ease is a confident mind, secure in itself, a storehouse of creativity rich with new ideas. A relaxed mind meets challenges with honor, respect and fearlessness, while a stressed mind is heavy and sees life as a burden. A mind stuck in an ego mind-set sees life as a competition. At any time we have the option to be in chaos or to be free by releasing the beliefs that are not serving us.

Let us not forget that life can be simple and wonderful. We have eyes that can see its vibrant colors, and ears that can hear its sweet sounds. May we appreciate the ground below our feet, the green grass, the smell of damp earth, the trees and the sky above us, the marvel of birds flying over, and the infinite magic of each precious moment. We always have the choice to live with dignity and wonder in the world, where the ordinary is really extraordinary.

The movement from a stressed mind to a relaxed one brings enormous relief. When we make the transition from a lack of confidence or little faith in ourselves to self-confidence and inner knowledge we see the power of mindful relaxation. Where the stressed mind lacks purpose, a relaxed mind sees meaning in all things.

We tend to think that the opposite of stress is passivity, that all we need do in order to relax is become inactive, like lying back on a beach chair. But passivity isn't the opposite of stress. Rather, we can attain an active and vibrant state where we are totally dynamic and totally relaxed at the same time. Then we can deal with life's demands without being drained or depleted, as we have a natural resource that keeps us in a state of balance and alertness. By using Yoga Nidra, we may appear passive, but within us there is total awareness of all things.

5

THE RELAXATION EFFECT

I learned the practice of Yoga Nidra at a yoga ashram in India, both in class and alone with the yoga master. I soon realized that Yoga Nidra led to a state of profound relaxation, and it has been with me ever since.

Before I went to India I thought that sensory diversion was the way to lessen stress, as is the norm in our culture that engages in a cycle of work and consumerism. Instead I learned a traditional method derived from the ancient Indian scriptures that enabled me to consciously relax with total awareness. I found it a fascinating discovery that the activities most people think of as relaxation often cause more tension!

I have taught Yoga Nidra to the executive vice president and CEOs of a major corporation in the United Kingdom and Europe. The BBC filmed me teaching Yoga Nidra to a football team in their locker room in England. I've taught Yoga Nidra to a member of the US Ski Team, and to members of a ski patrol in a cabin on top of a mountain. I taught a schoolteacher, who in turn taught his pupils, and he watched them become more spontaneous, saw their memories improve and energy levels increase. I've taught it to inmates in a prison, where each week more of them attended the class, finding that as they learned how to relax the easier it was to deal with their situations. I've used it with surgery patients and pregnant women. It's especially helpful in dealing with insomnia; if practiced just before going to bed it will induce a sound sleep.

Yoga Nidra and the state of being mindfully relaxed that ensues, enable us to transcend the patterns and reactions of the mind so we can deal with confusion, stress and frustration. From our original state of ease has come dis-ease; now we are moving toward a state of ease again. It is a flowing inward journey. Just as we can rearrange our house to correspond to our lifestyle, so we can make a positive difference in the internal structure of our being. Rather than being ruled by impulses, we can take charge and consciously "clean house," creating the environment anew, as beneath disorder our nature is innately calm and tranquil. We just have to learn how to access such peace. This is where Yoga Nidra enters the picture.

The Relaxation Response

Most of us think of relaxation as reading the newspaper, having a glass of wine or watching a movie. We may get a dog so we have to walk more, join a fitness club or take painting classes. Certainly these activities help us de-stress, but too often they deal only with the more superficial, immediate levels of stress and not with the more unconscious levels. They make us feel better for a while, until the next deadline or traffic jam begins to push us over the edge again.

Being mindfully relaxed enables us to go deeper within where we can release the unconscious levels of stress that affect both our behavior and health. As we have seen, a huge number of illnesses are caused by stress. This means a very large proportion of visits to doctors are stress-related, yet the medical world has no remedies, no prescription drugs that can change the events in our lives. We have to become our own physician and healer as change will only come through our own conscious efforts.

The relaxation response occurs when we can stay in touch with our inner being—with an inner sanctuary of peace—no matter what is happening around us. Then we respond to situations without the red flag waving, without adrenalin and cortisol coursing through the body, and without fear or panic. This is a state of deep psychological and physiological rest, which affects every part of us: metabolism is not shut down, heart rate doesn't increase, blood pressure stays normal, breathing remains calm. The sympathetic nervous system activity is decreased (this is associated with fight-or-flight responses) while the parasympathetic system (associated with relaxation) is increased, thereby releasing tense muscles and slowing excessive nervous activity. Alpha and theta brainwave activity is slowed, and a crossover is made from using the logical left side of the brain to the intuitive right brain.

As deeper levels of inner stress are eased, so fear, anxiety, and hopelessness are decreased, while concentration, efficiency, memory, and creativity are increased. This means we have greater tolerance and generosity, self-confidence and self-esteem. Here all the physical, psychological and emotional aspects of our being are balanced and strengthened, the body's entire regenerative system is stimulated, and our sense of well-being and healing potential are increased. When energy is no longer being directed toward hyperarousal, we have more energy and vitality available. Just as we care for our material possessions, so we can care for our greatest possession of all: our own precious being.

In a stressed state it's easy to lose touch with compassion and kindness, to focus instead on self-survival and competitiveness. It takes a relaxed state to connect with a deeper sense of purpose and our innate altruism. Yoga Nidra takes us beyond the discursive and distractive mind to the source of peace that is always in us, while mindfulness expands our understanding by freeing us from the habitual and often destructive patterns that control our lives and replacing them with a greater ease and simplicity.

Cultivating the Relaxed Mind

As we have seen, the stress response is largely due to how we respond to a situation, which is dependent on our perception, attitudes, inner state of mind and beliefs. The power of thought is such that if we think we are getting stressed or overwhelmed we'll be more likely to induce the stress response, while if we think easeful and calming thoughts we will induce the relaxation response. This makes a significant difference in our communication and relationships. For instance, in a stressed state we can get irritated or overwhelmed by relatively unimportant events, such as a child interrupting our conversation, or getting caught in traffic and being late for a meeting. In an easeful and relaxed state, we can view such disturbances for what they are without letting them cause unnecessary irritation. Rather than focusing on a minor and temporary inconvenience we are able to see the bigger picture.

A dysfunctional attitude makes our whole world dysfunctional: as we think, so we become. A stressed mind creates greater tension and chaos, while a calm and clear mind is able to think things through and create more positive solutions. When we are stressed everything is a challenge or an irritation, friendships can be lost and families broken, and we may even blame others for their shortcomings. In contrast, a relaxed mind is accepting, kind, and spontaneous, forgiving of others' failings; rather than getting caught up in analyzing details, it sees beyond the immediate situation to a state of balance. Our lives go from overwhelming to workable. By making a shift in our awareness we can move away from greed and selfishness toward generosity and compassion.

Just as a child acts with complete unaffectedness and spontaneity, so adults also possess that inner freedom; before we were dis-eased there must have been a time when we were at ease. And although our authentic state is one of ease, we have lost our direction and can't find the map. Restoring that original balance means being willing to move out of habitual patterns and see our world with an open mind. As the philosopher William James said, "Genius means little more than the faculty of perceiving in an unhabitual way."

Committing to Relaxation

Although stress is a major issue that affects health, relationships, families, and work, and even though we *say* we really do want to relax, we rarely give it proper consideration or time. Being creatures of habit accustomed to our existing, likely frenetic routine, we may think we are not the "relaxing type." Our unconscious patterns are strong motivators, even when intellectually we know an ongoing behavior is damaging, such as excessive drinking. Old habits are not easy to break, especially when they are the result of stress. We perpetuate mindless activities because we're unaware of how easily we could access the creative power of a quiet and relaxed mind.

Not having enough time to practice relaxation is undoubtedly the most common reason why we don't do it; trying to fit more into an already over-filled schedule seems impossible, there doesn't seem to be any space for the quiet time needed to connect with ourselves. Yet this very busyness is invariably what signals that relaxation needs to be our top priority.

We have to ask ourselves, honestly—is this how we want to be? It's very simple. No one can change our lifestyle other than ourselves. We are the only ones who can make a commitment to our sanity, to a deeper appreciation of life, to our health and happiness, to our peace of mind. The world will always be full of distractions, of things that need to be done, of demands and expectations, so it's up to us to make positive changes.

One of the biggest hurdles we have to overcome when justifying taking time for ourselves is guilt. Do you deserve to have time just for yourself? Perhaps the easiest way to look at this is to observe what happens when you *don't* take that time. Do you get resentful, tired, irritated, short-tempered, upset, or feel worthless and unappreciated? Do you lose your sense of humor, your patience, tolerance, and joy? And if any of this is true, is depriving yourself of "me time" really helping you at all?

Far from being selfish, taking time for ourselves is one of the most selfless things we can do. When we develop the relaxation response it improves both our attitudes and the quality of our caring, we create a more peaceful, respectful and loving environment for those around us. Our friends, family, and coworkers all benefit. Instead of feeling guilty because we are angry or exhausted, we'll be able to share more quality time together and give more to others.

To create a habit of practicing Yoga Nidra, we may need to get up earlier in the morning, take an hour out in the early evening or relax during lunchtime, but it's worth prioritizing the need to be relaxed. Normally we do everything else first, like washing dishes, shopping or making phone calls, while putting our own needs last. Yet enhancing and uplifting our mental state is surely the most important "to do" item of all.

With relaxation as a priority, our sanity is seen as more important than the laundry or the phone. Unless we look after our physical, mental and emotional health, we will be of little use to anyone, let alone ourselves. We must develop genuine respect for ourselves and act accordingly. A stressed mind will see life as overwhelming and unmanageable, but when we take time for ourselves we rediscover life as a wondrous and exciting adventure.

This is why commitment to a practice of Yoga Nidra and the relaxation it brings is so important; it is a commitment to ourselves, our stability, our tolerance, and our peace of mind. Let's make well-being our chief priority! Below are some questions to guide you in the right direction.

TIME-OUT: *Commitment*

This exercise helps you get clear on your commitments. Find a quiet place to sit with some paper and a pen. Take a few moments to settle, relaxing your body and deepening your breathing. When you are ready, ask yourself these questions:

- *What happens when I don't have time to myself? How do I behave? How do my body and mind react?*
- *Do I affect other people in a negative way? Do I blame them for making me stressed?*
- *Is well-being something I really want to achieve?*
- *Is relaxation on my list of priorities?*
- *Do I believe peace of mind is more important than anything else?*
- *Am I convinced that I can be at peace?*
- *Am I prepared to make changes?*

6

STARTING TO RELAX

We can begin the relaxation process by first bringing awareness to how we react to stress. For instance, we particularly need to pay attention when stress levels start to rise, and to how stress shows itself—perhaps as breathing gets shorter or the abdominal muscles tighten, a headache develops, we get short-tempered, or have a growing sense of hopelessness, frustration or confusion. If we focus enough awareness on any one of these symptoms we'll be able to release the stress and elicit the relaxation response. Any of the following methods can be used to start releasing the inner tension.

Breathe Deeply

Breathing happens automatically without our intervention. It is a constant, yet we are mostly unconscious of it. When we choose to breathe with conscious awareness we can use the breath to focus and relax more deeply, especially during stressful or emotional times. If stress levels are rising and demands become overwhelming, the first place this shows is in our breathing, as it will become faster, shallower and only engage the upper part of the chest. We have a different type of breath for each feeling, such as happiness, sadness, anger or fear, as the way we breathe corresponds directly to our emotions. Just by changing how and where we breathe can change how we feel.

Most spiritual traditions teach awareness of the breath as the foundation of relaxation and meditation techniques, as breathing internalizes awareness by bringing our attention inward. Being attentive to the natural flow of inhaling and exhaling centers awareness in the body, and the rhythm of our breathing helps us be fully present in the moment. All we need do is pay attention and watch the flow of the breath without trying to change it in any way or to impose control. Think of breathing as an anchor that holds us in the present.

The next time you begin to feel stress try to consciously breathe, longer and slower than normal, for three to five breaths. In this way you can let go of stress before a meeting, when someone wants a favor from you, when the children are winding you up, or when your mother-in-law calls with questions that try your patience. Use it to take the heat out of a situation, to steady quaking nerves or just be at ease. Mindful breathing is like a near and dear friend, always dependable and available to access greater calm.

When you first breathe like this it's quite natural to find yourself breathing erratically, perhaps faster or slower, or even to momentarily stop breathing. No matter. It is about intent, not perfect execution. Just breathe one breath at a time and stay focused on the flow of the breath and the sensation in the body. Or try one of the exercises below.

TIME-OUT: *Full Breathing*

This method will show you how breathing is affected by emotions. Find a quiet place to sit with a straight back and eyes closed. If it's easier, you can do this lying on the floor, as this relaxes the abdomen so you can breathe more deeply.

1.   *Start by breathing only into the upper part of your chest, just below your collarbone. The breath will be short and quick; it usually goes with feelings of fear, panic or anxiety. People who are very stressed usually breathe here most of the time.*

2. *Now breathe into the area below your heart, around your upper abdomen. This area usually feels calmer and safer, and the breath is slower although still slightly stressed.*

3. *Now breathe into your lower abdomen, about an inch below your navel. The breath here will be long and deep; it usually feels very relaxing, calm and centered.*

4. *Now join these three levels in one long breath. Start by breathing in at the top of the chest . . . fill the middle . . . and then fill the belly . . . pause, and then empty the belly . . . middle . . . and the top. Repeat the exercise three times.*

5. *Now reverse the process by breathing into and filling the belly . . . then the middle . . . and then the top of the chest . . . pause, and then empty the top . . . the middle . . . and the belly. Repeat three times, then relax.*

Spend a few minutes each day breathing through these three levels. It will help you relax more deeply.

TIME-OUT: *Mindful Throat Breathing*

This is one of the most relaxing breathing techniques of all, known as ujai pranayama in yoga. It can be done anytime, anywhere, with eyes open or closed, either sitting, standing or lying down. Breathing takes place in the throat at the well of the neck from the inside, and has a wonderfully soothing effect, instantly releasing tension throughout the whole body.

Bring your full awareness to the throat region and breathe in and out, focusing your mind at the well of your neck. Breathe from the throat to the navel and back. Continue for a few minutes until you are relaxed.

TIME-OUT: *Soft Belly*

Find a comfortable place to sit with your back straight and your eyes closed. Breathe a full inhalation, filling your lungs as deeply as you can, and blowing it out through your mouth, imagining it is blowing away tension.

Now breathe deeply into your belly, silently repeating: "soft belly, soft belly, soft belly." As your breath fills your belly let it soften any tension that is there. You can't stay in a stressed place when your belly is relaxed. Repeat three times.

Now breathe into the area of your heart—the heartspace—and feel your breath softening any resistance. Silently repeat: "soft heart, soft heart, soft heart." Breathe out tension; breathe in kindness and compassion. Repeat three times, then return to your normal breathing.

Take a deep breath and let it go, then open your eyes. Repeat this as often as you like.

Think Creatively

As your level of stress rises, do your thoughts become more upset, self-centered, panicked or fearful? If you normally react by getting irritated at interruptions until you start shouting, try taking some deep breaths and repeat, *"My world is flowing and easeful. My heart is open and loving."* Alternatively, you may find you are feeling increasingly helpless and inadequate. In this case, turn your thoughts into ones such as *"I am able to fulfill any request made of me; I am resourceful and can happily rise to this challenge."*

These techniques may seem too simple, but they work! Affirmations and mantras are not a way of denying reality; they aren't saying that everything is wonderful when obviously it's not. Affirmations simply help us move out of repetitive and negative mental patterns into healthy and creative ones. They might not remove the cause of stress, but will help us deal with stress in a more constructive way by reminding us that we are basically good, sane, and healthy, that we really are loving and caring.

Yet so often we affirm our weaknesses, failings or faults! We think things like, "I'm no good at this," "I'll never get it right," "I'm just so hopeless," or "I can't stop getting angry," which only serve to instill even stronger feelings of hopelessness or anger. The more we confirm our negative states, the more negative we will become, constantly putting ourselves down, undermining our capabilities and worthiness. This can happen so easily. Will I succeed? What will happen if I fail? As soon as we set out to do something, we are confronted by all the fear that holds us back.

Affirmations train the unconscious mind to shift these negative patterns, while energizing and motivating us to a greater capacity than we think we are capable of. They are a way to cut through conditioned behavior and connect us with our authentic selves. Furthermore, when we repeat an affirmation, any issues resisting it will arise; our negative behavior is highlighted because it is in conflict with the behavior we are affirming. For instance, if we resolve to become more caring and loving, it will be more apparent to us when we behave in an uncaring or unloving way.

Making an affirmation is a reminder of our intent in the deepest part of ourselves, an expression of who we really are beneath and beyond any limitations. It can be repeated at any time, silently or out loud—just prepare to feel wonderful! For instance, *My body is released and relaxed; my heartbeat is normal; my mind is calm and peaceful; my heart is open and loving.*

Imagine Freely

Whatever thoughts, attitudes or images we have in our minds will be felt in our bodies as if they are real. For example, if your thoughts are ones of not being able to cope, fear of the future, or depression about your financial situation, your body may well interpret these thoughts as life threatening and increase the stress response in preparation for fight-or-flight. Simply by changing the content of your mind you can change the state of your health and your sense of well-being. Visualization is the perfect way to do this.

Just for a moment, close your eyes and imagine yourself running. Then notice if this causes a corresponding stretching in your leg muscles; or imagine you are eating a slice of lemon and notice the saliva increase in your mouth. Now imagine you are standing beside a beautiful waterfall cascading down a steep embankment, the cool spray falling on your face. Stay with this image for a few minutes and then see how you feel. Relaxed?

Visualizing a beautiful or peaceful scene triggers the relaxation response through the release of endorphins, while increasing feelings of tranquility, love, inner strength and peace. It eases inner tension and uplifts our emotions.

To use visualization for stress release it's important to use images that are simple, free of too much detail, soothing and safe: images of floating in gentle waves lapping the shore or of lying in a field of wildflowers are ideal for overworked brains. If the imagery is too complicated it will engage too much mental energy. The relaxation will be deeper the more we let go of resistance and surrender to the image.

Visualization can also be used to ask our inner self for guidance and help, through imagining a meeting with a wise being. All the knowledge we need is already within us; the visualization enables us to tap into this wisdom and bring it into the conscious mind. Develop a peaceful image, such as walking through a wood or along a beach. Take time to relax. In this way you will enter more deeply into the unconscious.

You can practice visualization at any time, using it as a relaxation method on its own, or incorporating it into the Yoga Nidra practice (see Chapter 12). Either way, the images will release unconscious resistance and tension, while deepening your sense of easefulness. Here are two visualizations for you to try:

TIME-OUT: *Creative Visualization*

Use this exercise to create your own visualization. Find a comfortable place to sit or lie down, then notice your natural breathing and relax for a few minutes before you start. Eyes are closed.

Begin by imagining a perfect place in nature, somewhere very beautiful and peaceful. You feel welcomed here, you know you belong and are safe. Create the image of this place: see the colors, hear the sounds, feel the sun, touch the ground, explore the landscape. Are there birds or other animals here? Are there lakes, forests or mountains?

In this place you can put aside your concerns, your fears, all the nagging details of your life, and just be yourself. Nothing else is going on. Just let yourself be here, feel the quiet and the peace. Sometimes you may meet another being, perhaps an animal, a bird, or even a person. These represent aspects of your inner wisdom, so if they come ask them for guidance or healing.

When you are ready, take a deep breath, stretch, and roll over before you sit up. You can come back to this place whenever you choose for as long as you like; it is always with you because it is within you.

TIME-OUT: *Journey to Your Inner Truth*

Start by finding a comfortable place and either sit or lie down, with eyes closed, then notice your breathing and relax for a few minutes before you start.

Now imagine you are walking beside a lake, the sun warming you, the water a clear azure blue. All around are mountains and tall trees. You are alone here but you feel wonderfully safe, as if being held in the palm of a hand. It is so warm and safe that you take off your clothes and enter the water, your body able to swim and play, the water revitalizing your whole being. You enjoy the beauty of the sunlight catching the splashes, as you float and merge with the gentle rhythm of the water.

As you swim further into the lake you notice a cascading waterfall on the far side, falling over rocks and ferns into deep pools. You swim to the waterfall and stand beneath the cascading water, then dive into the pools. You hear the water splashing, and smell the freshness.

Then you notice beyond the waterfall a cave with a gentle light glowing within. The closer you get, the stronger the light becomes. The sweet smell of incense is in the air. In the center you see a large crystal, glowing with pure white light. It seems to welcome you inside, as if you are expected there. Beside the crystal sits a wise old woman, quietly smiling. Silently you sit beside her, the light illuminating you, a great warmth embracing your body.

The wise woman speaks words of healing for you. In response you share your heart, your troubles, your dreams. She offers guidance and words of wisdom. Then she hands you a crystal that you hold to your heart. This crystal will always be with you as a source of strength.

You stay a few moments more before rising and making your way onto the bank above the lake. There you find new clothes waiting for you, the softest of clothes that feel like silk. As you walk back along the edge of the lake you pass your old clothes, discarded on the shore. You do not need them anymore; they are the past.

Let the visualization fade. Take a deep breath and spend a few moments breathing and reconnecting. Open your eyes, then stretch your legs and arms. When you are ready, roll on your side, sit up and greet your world.

7

MAKING FRIENDS
WITH OURSELVES

When we are mindfully relaxed we can make friends with ourselves and become our own ally; this is a marriage of the body and mind, an embracing of ourselves just as we are. Yet instead of fostering such friendship for ourselves, many of us deny our feelings, dislike our body, or think we are full of faults with few redeeming qualities. We feel shameful, unworthy, or get easily irritated and upset with ourselves. These are the very issues we can work with and transform. If we are not at peace with ourselves, we can't be at peace with anyone else. Making friends with who we are, just as we are, is a vital step to inner peace and happiness. And when we accept ourselves, we can also more easily accept others.

We can start by gaining an overview of how we see ourselves, getting in touch with the various labels we use to define ourselves. For instance, we identify with the race we were born to or the country where we were born: I'm English, I'm African American, I'm Jewish from Austria, etc. We also identify ourselves through our religion, often feeling a separation from—if not hostility toward—those who follow a different path.

We also gain an identity through work. As children we are often asked what we want to be when we grow up, as if our work label becomes who we are: I'm a doctor, I'm a teacher, I'm a bus driver. Alongside this is the sense of failure, guilt or worthlessness if we don't become what was expected of us, if we don't succeed at attaining our work label.

These are the big labels we use to define our identity, but there are also many smaller ones that influence our behavior and attitudes. Some of them give us an emotional identity, such as mother, divorcée or recovering alcoholic. Then there are the more personal labels, the many ways we see ourselves: weak, strong, unworthy, worried, intelligent, stupid, hopeless, and so on.

Recognizing all the different ways we identify ourselves—all the masks we assume or the fake selves we project in order to come across in a certain way—is vital in our journey to release stress, gain peace and understand ourselves more deeply. Do you switch from one label to another during the day, keeping the real you hidden? Beneath the label, who is there? Do you know this person?

When we label something we put it in a box; it is now known, dealt with, and we can store it away without further enquiry. Which is what we often do with those parts of ourselves we don't want to know anymore.

Do you identity more with the surface content of your life, rather than the essence of who you really are? Can you find yourself without the masks, without all the ways you present yourself? When we identify with the masks, we lose sight of what lies beneath them. But the labels are only a part of us, not the whole, and we need to know and honor our whole being.

TIME-OUT: *Noting and Labeling*

Find a comfortable place to sit quietly. Have a pen and paper with you. Take some deep breaths and feel your body relaxing and settling.

Begin by making a list of all the big labels that define you, starting with the ones that are most obvious, such as your race, age, parent, child, sibling, gender, religion, occupation, hair color, and so on. Build a list that would tell the outside world who you are in superficial terms.

Then make a list of all your emotional and mental labels: how you see yourself and how you think others see you, whether you are an angry or a caring person, ambitious or shy.

Then list the ways you hide your real self, the masks you use to present an image to the world, the masks that you hide behind. This may be the hardest to write. Just be honest with yourself.

Relax for a moment before you look at your list. Read it through a few times and see if you can find yourself as more than a list of descriptors or masks. Are there ways this inner you can find expression in your life? Can you begin to let go of the labels and the masks?

Then take a deep breath and release the arbitrary boxes, labels and roles that have been defining you. Let yourself simply be, rather than needing to associate yourself with particular societal or personal expectations. Who is there? Welcome and make friends with this person. Keep the list for future reference.

Self-Acceptance

If we are to heal our body and mind from the effects of stress, then we need to infuse every part of ourselves with awareness and acceptance. Making friends with ourselves means seeing and embracing everything, the good and the not so good. It means seeing ourselves as we are, not as we would like to be, including how we judge our behavior, looks or feelings, and noticing how easily we feel embarrassed or ashamed of ourselves.

All the ways we dismiss our feelings and judge ourselves create tension and disturb our peace. We resist intimacy so that nobody can get close enough to really know us; we keep ourselves so busy that we avoid confrontation with our inner selves; or we bury our feelings deep inside in the hope they will somehow just disappear.

Some of us were raised to believe it is immodest or even self-centered to think well of ourselves. Yet self-acceptance is not self-obsession; it's feeling at ease with who we are. We can't be six feet tall when we are five feet four, we can only be ourselves, and self-acceptance lies in seeing the beauty in our uniqueness. We need to focus on our relationship to ourselves, on discovering our place in the world, and on a confidence and dignity in our right to be here. Everything we do, everything we feel, all our attitudes and thoughts, stem from this sense of being and belonging. If we feel unsure of ourselves, uneasy in our world, or lacking in confidence, then we are like a small bird flitting from one branch to another, startled by the slightest sound; when we are at ease within ourselves with a greater sense of self-acceptance, we will be more relaxed and at ease in our world.

Is a caterpillar any less beautiful or captivating than a butterfly? Or is it equally fascinating and exquisite? When we can truly accept and appreciate the inherent beauty in ourselves we will naturally evolve into a more relaxed and comfortable place. Developing a positive self-image, greater self-esteem or confidence doesn't mean we are full of our own self-importance. Rather, when we make friends with ourselves just as we are, those are the natural by-products.

TIME-OUT: *Self-Acceptance*

Take a few minutes for yourself, find a comfortable place to sit, then breathe deeply and relax your body. Have the list of your labels and masks with you that you made earlier.

Now review the list and highlight those attributes that you have trouble accepting. Choose one of them to focus on. It might be a trait like impulsivity or something about your physical appearance. Close your eyes and allow your mind to explore all your feelings about this part: its history, how it has affected your life, how it has limited or aided your relationships, happiness or activities. Really get to know it.

Now be aware of how you judge this part. See if you can find where those feelings of judgment come from. Who told you that you were unacceptable? Your parents, your partner or society? Does this part of you feel cold, lonely, unwanted or rejected?

Try to simply suspend or let go of any judgment for a moment. Bring this part of you into your heart and give it love. Can you see it as an integral part of your being that needs to be embraced and cared for? With each breath feel your heart opening ever more deeply to accepting yourself just as you are.

When you are ready, take a deep breath and gently stretch.

Overcoming Obstacles

Fear, anxiety, anger and other negative emotions are obstacles on our path to inner peace; they are as much a cause of stress as by-products of it. Becoming fearful about an impending deadline, for instance, can cause anxiety and raise intolerance levels with outbursts of temper, while increasing a sense of separation from others as we find ourselves in an ever more isolated place.

We are rarely without fear as it accompanies us every time we enter a new or unknown situation. Fear that arises in response to perceived danger is natural and protective. But fear based on the *possibility* of something happening, on the *thought* of failing or an *imagined* future will continually limit our confidence, personal power and capability.

Anxiety arises in response to feeling powerless or when circumstances become uncontrollable, such as being stuck in traffic on the way to an important meeting, or in relation to others when we feel out of control and helpless. But, like fear, anxiety is often based on what *might* happen—on a future scenario—rather than on what is actually happening in the present.

Stress-related irritation and anger, or sudden outbursts of rage with little apparent cause, are often due to stress hormones flooding our system in response to feeling overwhelmed or unable to cope. How easily we blame others for our own sense of inadequacy! Anger is also the voice of the ego, an expression of righteous self-centeredness, a voice that easily grows in volume.

The more such stress-related issues dominate our behavior, the more essential it becomes to practice mindful relaxation, to save our sanity as well as our health and happiness. That way the obstacles—whether irritation, anger, fear or something more serious—can become stepping stones to greater self-understanding. In a relaxed state fear becomes fearlessness and confidence, while anxiety becomes acceptance and trust that all things will unfold in their own way. Anger is replaced by patience, tolerance and a deep letting go. Relaxation doesn't turn us into a doormat for everyone to step on, but we certainly become more amenable.

The important point is that negative emotions may be a part of the human condition but we needn't let them rule us. The aim of the exercise below is to develop an awareness of how and when an obstacle arises, and how it influences our behavior, thoughts or feelings. As this awareness deepens, we will no longer be victim to it; negativity loses its power when we face and make friends with it.

I have chosen to focus this exercise on fear, as it is often the most debilitating emotion; but the exercise can work equally well with anxiety, anger or any other stressful emotion that limits us. After a few days of practicing it, note if your responses are changing—like fear or anger arising less—or whether you are coping more effectively with anxiety. For instance, watch what happens to fear when you are no longer fearful of it. The breathing exercises and affirmations in the last chapter are also invaluable for transforming negative emotions.

TIME-OUT: *Transforming Obstacles into Stepping Stones*

Replace the word fear *with any other emotion you would like to release.*

Every day for a week carry a notepad and pen with you and become an observer of any fearful reactions to events. Whenever you feel fear arising, observe it carefully. Then ask yourself these questions:

- *What was happening before the fear arose?*
- *What triggered the fear? Was it a particular circumstance, person, a thought or a specific feeling?*

- *What physical effect did the fear have? Note any physical changes, such as sudden heat, cold, sweating, palpitations, stomach cramp, muscle ache or headache.*
- *What impact did the fear have on you mentally and emotionally? Did you get nervous, weepy, frightened, helpless, powerless or overwhelmed?*
- *What followed the fear?*
- *Did anxiety, anger or any other state arise?*
- *What happens when you try to confront your fear? Can you get to know it?*
- *Can you breathe into fear and let it go with each outgoing breath?*

When you are done, take a deep breath and relax. You are getting to know how fear affects you. Notice what happens the next time fear arises. You will still feel it, but with less intensity. It will be less dominating. Slowly it will become your friend.

8

MAKING FRIENDS WITH OTHERS

Isn't it extraordinary that relationships are the most rewarding and satisfying part of life, yet are also the biggest source of stressors? As much as we love each other, our personal issues are compounded by our expectations and the demands we make on our loved ones, causing endless confusion and misunderstanding. Our egos are constantly butting up against each other, causing tension and distress; we cling to our way of doing things versus someone else's way, and the need to hold on to what we think is the right way makes us dig our heels in. Different likes and dislikes, attractions and repulsions, mood swings, blaming and shaming can all create barriers to communicating clearly and freely. We misunderstand each other, causing conflicts to arise because what we say is not always what we mean. Or we hide behind our inhibitions, not knowing how to be honest about our feelings, but resenting our partner or friend for not intuiting our intentions.

When Deb and I had a private meeting with the Dalai Lama in India, his warmth and humor were contagious. As he sat holding our hands, I told him I didn't want to leave, I just wanted to be with him and learn from his wisdom. He surprised me by replying: "If we were together all the time we would quarrel!" What I learned from this is that we are all human!

Relationships are fundamental to our existence; we are in a constant relationship with ourselves, each other and the world around us. Any form of stress both influences and is influenced by the state of our relationships. Positive emotional support makes an enormous difference in our ability to deal with tension by providing a safe place in which to find comfort and reassurance. Any disruption to that foundation invariably makes it harder to cope, which is why separation, divorce and loneliness are all at the top of the list of the most stress-producing situations any of us have to face.

As relationships are so vital to our well-being, we need to maintain honesty and openness with those who are closest to us. If we ignore our feelings or pretend we are feeling differently than we are, not only do we avoid intimacy but we also create more isolation. Repressed feelings don't just disappear—they stay locked inside us and influence our attitudes and behavior. For instance, feelings of being misunderstood or mistrusted turn into resentment; resentment turns into anger, distress and even depression.

When stress becomes distress we tend to push others away and shut down our caring and sharing in an attempt to cope, becoming hard-hearted and unsympathetic. Awareness and mindfulness are the keys here: awareness of our feelings and where they're arising from, why they are affecting us so deeply, and mindfulness to bring about a peaceful resolution. Being honest about our feelings, while also respecting those of another, is essential to experiencing greater intimacy and love.

In an intimate relationship we allow someone to see us as we really are, which also demands a letting go of our defenses. For intimacy is *Into me you see!* and can only occur when we are willing to be genuinely true to ourselves and unafraid of being seen as such by another.

When we are at ease within ourselves, intimacy gives us the opportunity to enter into a depth of sharing and caring with another that dissolves the ego boundaries. But when stress levels are rising, intimacy can make us feel we have no space, no room for our own thoughts—we want to shut out the world and that includes those closest to us. Too easily we fall into patterns of guilt or blame, pitting our own requirements against our partner's, demanding that our needs be heard or attended to without acknowledging theirs. Or we sacrifice our feelings in order to make our partner happy, in the belief that our needs are less important, which fosters resentment.

If we don't fully apprehend that we are all connected, we'll believe we can hurt someone else and not be hurt ourselves; we don't see how their pain is also our pain, since it leaves us in a place of insecurity and isolation. In a deeply relaxed state we connect to others with a greater self-acceptance and inner ease, enabling us to deal more effectively with such issues as a lack of self-esteem or confidence, guilt or shame and insecurity, as we go beneath our normal self-preoccupation to a more spacious and loving place. We don't have to hold so tight to our ego's insistence on getting its way; we can let go, relax and still be safe.

Communicating and Sharing

Communication is vital to being alive. Through it we expand our understanding, deepen our connectedness, go beyond our separate selves into the minds and hearts of others, and know we are a part of something much greater than any one of us. Without communication we have wars, dysfunctional families, increased loneliness, marital breakdown and rising stress levels. Just through the tone of our voice and the words we use we can increase intimacy, safety and love, or we can cause hurt, rejection and conflict.

How often have you felt you weren't being heard? Conversely, how often do you actually hear what someone else is saying to you? And do you listen without judging, criticizing, or wanting to make it better, to "fix" what is being shared with you? Do you and your family have times of just talking together, expressing feelings, respecting and really honoring each other?

Communication is about sharing our feelings, as much as it is about being heard and really hearing someone else. It's a two-way experience and both sides are equally important: honesty in what we express and openness in receiving feedback. Responsibility means the "ability to respond"; to be responsible in this context is to be responsive to both ourselves and others, and to respond mindfully when someone communicates with us. While a reaction is a reflection of habitual behavior patterns, with little thought involved, a response reflects an awareness of all the elements present, not just our own subjective point of view. But when stress levels are rising we shut down the ability to both share and listen. This in turn engenders feelings of being unrecognized and unworthy, deep frustration, resentment and isolation.

Many of us find communication difficult because we don't know how to express our feelings. As children we may have been taught to keep our feelings to ourselves, to suffer in silence; perhaps our parents never really shared their feelings so we never learned how to do it; or perhaps we were never really listened to so we simply shut down. Sharing our feelings might be accompanied by shame or embarrassment, as if a secret hiding place has been exposed, or because we believe we have nothing worthwhile to say. However, the more we share, even if it's difficult at first, the less threatening sharing will become and the more deeply connected we will be to each other. As we find our voice, it will grow stronger and truer.

Stress, loneliness, feeling we are not being heard, recognized or loved isolates us. To truly listen is to receive another into ourselves, without judgment or criticism, without trying to make everything right. To truly share is a great relief, to be known and accepted by another, to be fully received. We no longer have to carry our story around with us but can safely put it down. It has been heard.

On the one hand we are each alone, unique, separate individuals, and yet at the same time we are not alone, we are all interconnected, walking the same earth and breathing the same air. There is an interrelationship between all things, all forms of life.

Find the place where you start or where your food starts or where your source of water starts. Can you find it? Or do you keep going from one connection to the next, from your body to your parents and then your grandparents, or from the loaf of bread to the baker, to the grain, to the rain and the sun and the earth? Are we separate from the food we eat or the water we drink? Is there anything that is independent or unconnected? Or is everything interconnected to something or someone else? I think you will agree we are all deeply interconnected.

Appreciating Our World

Stress can insulate us so much that we lose touch with the world around us, don't see the beauty and vibrancy of nature, and forget about caring for our environment. Yet relating to our world is vital for a sense of balance and wholeness. We are not separate entities, spinning in the whirlwind of our own small units; we are an integral part of a much larger picture, each of us connected to each other, to the earth, oceans and sky.

To reduce stress it is vital to take time to enjoy nature: take a walk through a park and smell the flowers or freshly cut grass, notice the pattern of a spider web sparkling with raindrops, or fill a window box with flowers so the colors brighten your view. Appreciating nature has the most wonderful effect on our state of mind.

Unfortunately, given the state of the world these days we can easily be overwhelmed by the immensity of what needs to be done to help our planet. Ignoring the problem by focusing only on ourselves solves nothing, it simply creates more problems. Instead, we must become the solution as an active participant in the health of our world. The pain of the earth is the pain of not being loved, cared for, respected or honored. When we bring healing to the environment it awakens our connectedness and compassion for all life. It expands us beyond ourselves and our immediate concerns, difficulties or pressures.

When we feel our connectedness we realize that even our thoughts have an impact, not just our actions. We are all co-creators of our world, and all forms of life are precious and meaningful. Instead of focusing on ourselves as the center of our universe, we benefit by perceiving that we are a part of a constantly changing, interrelated dynamic where no one is greater or lesser—we are all in it together.

The practice of *ahimsa*, which means noninjury, harmlessness or nonviolence in Sanskrit, empowers us to live fearlessly. Both Mahatma

Gandhi and the Dalai Lama beautifully exemplify the qualities of ahimsa; each made history by using nonviolent solutions to achieve their goals. These two great men, among many others, have shown how the power of compassion is far greater than that of the sword.

"The best soldier does not attack," wrote the Chinese philosopher Lao-Tzu. "The superior fighter succeeds without violence. The greatest conqueror wins without struggle. . . . This is intelligent nonaggressiveness."

We too can reach this state. Mindful relaxation relieves the distress of negative past impressions and clears out the storehouse embedded within us to create positive thoughts and motivations, so that we can direct our lives in a creative and spontaneous way. It is an attitude, a state of mind and a way of being. When our minds can be quiet and harmless, then peace becomes dynamic. We no longer need to feel helpless about the state of our world; we can cultivate the mind-set needed to bring about the world we want.

Through practical means and self-enquiry we can experience the wonders of our inner treasure house, the creative and intuitive marvel of an aware mind. Beyond our mind and intellect is an ocean of blissful consciousness that is vibrant, vital and more fulfilling than words can describe. Here we can communicate with others and respond to their needs and those of the planet with empathy and joy.

9

OPENING THE HEART

We live in a world filled with desire, greed and selfishness. How well most of us know this! The cause is our longing for our lives to be different, along with the inability to accept things as they are. We either pursue what we want like a dog chasing its tail, or try to avoid what we don't want; it's a never-ending cycle. Imagine, even billionaires never have enough! Such desire stops us from realizing the joy of deep relaxation, as it continually distracts us, yet it is also the very ground from which we can flourish, like roses that grow from compost.

The ego, while being both elusive and quite subtle, is also a self-centered, self-seeking, devious trickster that seduces us into wanting and grasping—what I call the "me-me syndrome." While it prevents us from seeing things clearly and objectively or from genuinely connecting to others, it also prevents us from being generous and compassionate. The ego is an enemy to relaxation. It is the obstacle that will distract us in all ways possible and create endless dramas. It will also do everything and anything it can to throw us into a state of confusion. But when we relax, we are able to transcend its demands.

The way out of this most demanding aspect of ourselves is through the practice of Yoga Nidra, which encourages caring, kindness, selflessness and humility, all hallmarks of a relaxed mind and all qualities we possess innately but which are hidden by ego delusions. Through Yoga Nidra we not only learn how to relax, but also how to connect with the capacity to transform ourselves from the inside out. Such transformation occurs naturally; as the inner stresses and tensions are released we discover our inherent peace of mind.

In a relaxed state we can transform a negative state into a positive one. Instead of reacting when something challenging happens, for instance, we can respond positively to remedy the situation, like spinning straw into gold. If someone insults us, it's invariably because of their feelings of stress or pain, so by responding with compassion rather than aggression or negativity, we avoid causing further hurt or insult. It's wonderful to be noninjurious, both for ourselves and the other person.

We don't need to put our own needs ahead of others, nor do we need to put them last. A balance can be achieved by acknowledging ourselves while also responding to and caring for the people in our lives. This means being responsible *in relation* to others; and as we begin to see more deeply, the heart naturally opens.

Many of us spend a lot of time protecting ourselves by ignoring, denying or hiding our feelings, pretending to be braver than we are, convincing ourselves we aren't good enough and denying the power of love. Now we can feel those rusty old gates opening wide, allowing the light to be revealed. The depth within the heart, the wealth of who we are, can no longer be hidden. Mindful relaxation fills our being and awakens us to the true heart.

In this way our lives begin to ease and change, for the real transformation is coming from within. Life may not be like calm water, but we can surf the waves and be unafraid to get our feet wet. We have the strength to overcome our difficulties; we can make a commitment to dive in, a commitment to release our ego-identity by surrendering to the open heart.

Unconditional Happiness

Our normal attitude to happiness is one of believing that it lies somewhere in the future, such as when we have more money, an ideal partner, a better job, when our children are married—then we can be happy. Do you believe you would be happier if you could go to a tropical island or if you lost some weight? Do you feel as if happiness is waiting for you one day, sometime, somewhere?

And if you do actually feel happy, can you trust it? If I have it today will it last till tomorrow? Many of us have been hurt, let down or had to struggle through difficulties, so our ability to trust happiness as something that will endure has been broken or destroyed. We are accustomed to life being stressful, even painful; we don't believe happiness will last but that more difficulties will soon follow. Happiness appears as unreliable, transient and impermanent.

We also have a hard time believing that we deserve happiness. Guilt and shame color our feelings—either guilt over our own actions, based on cultural norms that say we can't be happy until we have atoned for our sins or shame from past behavior that buries happiness inside. We believe we have to earn or pay for happiness in some way. How could we be innately worthy of being happy?

The beauty we discover through deep relaxation, as the inner layers of stress and guilt are released, is a natural joy arising. Where before there was anxiety or constant worries jostling for room in our minds, now there is spaciousness, an expansive and delicious peace. In just the half hour that we practice Yoga Nidra, we enter into this spacious deep quiet. And as that bliss and peace fill the whole of our being, with it comes happiness. Peace and happiness come hand and hand—an innate arising as we let go of struggle, resistance, fear, and isolation—and remain with us long after our relaxation session is over.

It's a wonderful revelation to realize that true happiness is inside, that it isn't dependent on anyone or anything outside of us, that we don't have to behave in a certain way, be rich or thin or married or successful in order to be happy. We can touch on a level of joy that is unconditional, that has no limitations or restrictions. As such happiness is an integral part of us, it must have always been there, waiting for us to connect with and open into it. A source of innate joy, a richness of spirit, is always there within each of us no matter what is happening in our lives, when we mindfully relax and pay attention.

Happiness is our birthright, our essence, the source of who we are—and we have every right to enjoy it. It is a natural expression of our being, the joy of life expressing itself through us. It is the earth that maintains its orbit, the sun and moon that radiate to all beings equally, the seasons that flow in their cycle nourishing us with beauty.

Loving-Kindness

The more the mind is relaxed, the wider the heart opens. As we move from a stressed state to a relaxed one we are also moving to loving-kindness, compassion and forgiveness, all qualities of a tender heart. With this comes a movement from self-centeredness to other-centeredness. The transformation frees us from the limitations of an ego-centered experience. We go from a negative relationship with ourselves to a caring and positive one, which invites these more altruistic qualities to become a natural expression of who we are.

We can live in this world as the lotus flower that rises from the mud with petals that are clean and untainted. Our mud is composed of the restrictions we can transform in order to see the light. By being mindfully relaxed we clear a way through the mud and enable deep change to occur, emerging free of our conditioned mind.

> **Generosity:** To give of ourselves for the sake of others, to give without needing anything in return, is true generosity. This is seen in the three traditional aspects of giving: the giving of things, the giving of loving protection and the giving of loving understanding. Yet how often do we give something in the hope or expectation that we will get something in return? Are we able to give freely and unconditionally? Are we able to experience the joy that is inherent in the act of giving? Generosity enables us to go beyond our limitations, to connect at the heart. This is a very precious gift. Even if you think you have nothing to give, you have the riches of a smile or a kind word.

> **Loving-Kindness and Compassion:** Such altruistic qualities may seem too lofty to achieve, but they are naturally within us—we don't

get them from somewhere outside. Deep within we know we have the capacity for great love, caring and compassion that goes beyond our individual selves. Thinking only of ourselves tends to isolate us further and create deeper loneliness. As soon as we open the heart to love, we are uplifted and deeply connected.

Forgiveness: This is not separate from love, as it arises as a natural manifestation of an open heart. Forgiveness doesn't mean ignoring something that was hurtful, or accepting the unacceptable—nor is it forgetting. But we can forgive ourselves or the other person by recognizing the fear, pain and confusion that was behind the act, and by recognizing our shared humanity. We are all capable of making mistakes, of hurting each other. Forgiveness is releasing our attachment to pain, to the ego story it tells, so we can love more deeply. We can forgive the person, whether we forgive the action or not. When we allow ourselves to forgive, instead of holding onto hurt, it is like a dam opening that releases our love, laughter and healing energies to make us whole again.

TIME-OUT: *Generosity, Kindness, and Forgiveness*

For a whole day make a point of saying hello or smiling at others, and watch what happens. See if it changes how you feel. Watch if fear arises, and especially if fear separates you from others. Notice that the more you smile the more smiles you receive.

Then for a whole day be kind and generous to yourself. Honor your own needs, watch those times you ignore your feelings and be even more generous at those times. Spend the day practicing random acts of kindness wherever you go, bringing kindness to your world.

Now practice forgiveness for a whole day. Forgiving yourself is just as important as forgiving others, so any time either you or someone else does or says something hurtful, take a deep breath and silently repeat, "I forgive you." Watch what happens to your feelings. The more you can forgive, the more you will release the distress and find a deeper peace.

10

Perceptions of Consciousness

Although our minds are full of endless chatter and drama, caught in the duality of success and failure or attraction and repulsion, there is always the potential for entering into the still and quiet place within. We cut through the many layers of misunderstanding by becoming aware of both the enslaving and unshakeable power of the ego; for when it is in control, it has us running round and round, totally distracted from the quiet space. Mindfulness renders the ego redundant by bringing us into a deeper state of awareness, showing how the egoic mind is a perfect servant but a terrible master. Once we recognize self-righteous thoughts and actions, and see them as the self-deceptions they really are, they no longer have power over us.

Through mindful relaxation we open to the exquisite vastness of consciousness. The following story is of a great yogi and his ardent disciple. One time the guru told his disciple they should meet at the local park at noon the following day. The seeker was prompt and waited patiently for some time, but to his dismay his master never showed. He was disappointed and left, wondering what the teaching might be. The next time he was with his guru he asked why he had not come to the park as planned. The teacher replied: "You need to practice more. I was hiding behind the rays of the sun!" This illustrates the subtle depth of consciousness behind everything that we can all experience, the richness there is to discover. Within us there is a fountain of joy and an ocean of bliss!

To know what is real we need to recognize what is unreal; to know truth we need to be truthful with ourselves. For me, mindfulness is a conscious emptying rather than a filling up. Our wisdom has been hidden by countless dramas and endless issues—our mud—and now it can be cleared away to uncover the pristine flower beneath. We can release repetitive thoughts, selfish desires, as well as all the accumulated, countless stories the ego mind creates, gently letting them all go. The depth of our insight into the dimensions and perceptions of consciousness is a result of our willingness to open to the discovery of new possibilities and ways of being. Enlightenment, the realization of our authentic nature, is already within us and through deep relaxation and self-enquiry it is revealed.

This is why relaxation is so vital. It makes the journey from the external world of the senses to the inner world of peace possible. The process of withdrawing the mind and senses is one of moving from the gross to the sublime, as our consciousness becomes ever more subtle. The practice itself may or may not awaken self-realization, but it creates the opportunity and environment in which awakening can occur naturally.

The Five Bodies or Koshas

When we refer to the dimensions of the mind in Western psychology we talk of the conscious, subconscious and unconscious. Eastern terminology calls them the gross, subtle and casual dimensions. Out of these three dimensions there are five bodies or *koshas*. Each one is an ever-finer level of awareness.

This approach offers us an expansive perspective for understanding the dimensions of consciousness. Mindful relaxation directly and positively affects them, and as all five koshas are interconnected, so by bringing awareness to one we benefit from them all.

1. *Annamaya*, known as the food body, is our physical body, comprised of the organs, tissues, skeleton and fluids, and all that

is absorbed through our senses. It represents the grossest level and is perceived as our outer body. This is where we can immediately feel the effect of relaxation as muscles relax, tension subsides and a greater ease is felt throughout—this is where the practice of Yoga Nidra starts. By knowing and inhabiting the body we will feel more present and easeful.

2. *Pranayama*, the energy or prana body that permeates annamaya, consists of the energy systems in the body, such as breathing, digestion, excretion, circulation, immunity, and so forth. Known as the vital force or chi, this kosha is positively affected by breathing exercises that increase our prana, and by relaxation that releases any resistance limiting the flow of energy in our body.

3. *Manomaya*, the mental body, relates to all the mental processes from creativity and imagination to perception and belief; it is the kosha responsible for our nervous system, mind and emotions. Affirmations and relaxation bring clarity and ease to this kosha, releasing anxiety and obsessive thinking while creating a calm mental and emotional space.

4. *Vijnanamaya*, the higher mind, wisdom or psychic body, is the source of our inner knowing, intuition and insight. Relaxation increases this kosha through objective witness awareness, where we go beyond our ego identification to our inner truth.

5. *Anandamaya*, the bliss body, is the deepest part of us that is filled with tenderness, contentment, joy and the bliss beyond duality; it is the sense of coming home to our true selves. Relaxation enables us to dive into this bliss.

The Chakras or Levels of Consciousness

An important way to experience the many dimensions of our being is through the chakras or levels of consciousness. They may be likened to energy gateways within our being through which we connect with greater states of awareness that influence and enrich our perception of reality. The chakras are not physical, but can be accessed by focusing the mind at specific points along the spinal region.

There are seven major chakras, each defining a different aspect of the development and awakening of consciousness. They are centers of subtle energy sometimes depicted as energy vortexes in the body, as spinning wheels, linked with a specific color or sound, or even as lotus flowers with many petals. And just as a lotus grows from mud and emerges pristine in the sun, so the chakras symbolize our growth from the realms of darkness or ignorance to the exquisite light of enlightenment, moving from below the base of the spine upward to the top of the head. This reflects the movement from instinctive, self-centered behavior through the expression of the ego, to the highest state of divine wisdom.

1. *Muladhara or Root Chakra.* This first chakra is about survival, security and self-preservation, as well as our ancestral and family history, a sense of belonging and personal validity. It is the storehouse of all past impressions and experiences, our *samskaras*, and is where our deepest fears are buried.

An inactive muladhara means we will cower in the face of problems, are unable to cope or provide, both financially and emotionally. Fear of survival makes us suspicious and greedy, with an "I come first" attitude. We may also feel as if we don't belong, receive no support from loved ones or can't trust anyone; we may even feel suicidal. Conversely, an active muladhara enables us to positively meet survival challenges, and our attitude is accepting and trusting of others. We feel secure and confident in our world.

The lotus grows from the mud and this chakra represents the very deepest level of mud. It is here that the flower begins its journey upward to the sunlight. This chakra is the root or foundation of the chakra system and is accessed at the perineum.

2. *Swadhisthana or Sacral Chakra.* This second chakra relates to the unconscious. It moves from the awareness of survival to that of

procreation and the realm of desire, which gives rise to the duality of pleasure and pain, keeping us bound to physical existence. Having secured our ground we now need to deal with the details of living, which includes both procreation and finances.

If the energy of the second chakra is inactive then we will have low sexual desire, feel helpless or unable to cope. Sexual energy is often misused, which can make us feel guilty, shamed, confused and deceived. We may also have poverty consciousness or feel inadequate financially. This is symptomatic of feeling devalued or losing self-esteem. When swadhisthana is open we feel balanced and at ease, whether in our relationships with others or in our financial circumstances, and not ruled by our unconscious desires. Swadhisthana is accessed at the base of the spine.

3. *Manipura or Solar Plexus Chakra.* This third chakra awakens the perception of self-identity and ego, which include the fierce energies of power and control. It is connected to the solar plexus. From survival and procreation, we come to the development of the individual I, self-consciousness and personal power.

Manipura is focused on the ego and is directly associated with fear, rage and all the other issues pertaining to control and power. When inactive it gives rise to a false sense of authority, with delusions of grandeur that cloud awareness. Its consciousness wants to dominate others and is highly ambitious, with a desire for wealth, power and exploitation, as in the energy of dictators, leaders, politicians, athletes and entertainers, even of psychics. But it also includes a fear of power, of trusting others, as well as the inability to make our own decisions—instead needing to be told what to do.

An active third chakra enables us to have a positive and self-assured sense of personal power, inner authority and emotional strength, without needing to exert control over others. We feel worthy, valuable and confident. The exercise of will is normally associated with ego-centeredness and achievement, but here also lies the seed for enlightenment—the desire to awaken, to go beyond the ego—and once it's awakened, this is a very powerful energy. Manipura is accessed at the level of the navel in the spine.

4. *Anahata or Heart Chakra.* This fourth chakra is known as the heart chakra due to its connection with our center of love and compassion. Moving from the development of the individual at the third chakra, we now expand beyond our selfish needs to opening the heart to qualities of kindness and caring; we go from self-centeredness to other-centered awareness.

A closed heart chakra is an unfeeling or cold heart, unable to express caring, based either in sensuality or rationality with a lack of warmth or altruism. We may feel unlovable, fear being hurt or exposed or unable to forgive, attitudes engendering untold misery; there may be bitterness, jealousy, deep sorrow or hard-heartedness.

An open-heart chakra is an infinite source of love and compassion; the more the heart opens, the more we are filled with love. It awakens us to a real love for ourselves that brings true forgiveness and freedom, and a genuine and profound loving-kindness and compassion for all beings. Here we awaken truly human awareness and the development of unconditional love toward all. Anahata can be accessed at the impression of the chest in the spinal cord.

5. *Vishuddhi or Throat Chakra.* This fifth chakra is the center of purification and communication, speaking truth and tasting the nectar of wisdom. From an awareness of others and the development of loving-kindness, our true voice is expressed. In Indian mythology the swan with its graceful long neck represents this chakra, as the swan can discriminate between milk and water just as the yogi can discriminate between truth and ignorance.

Vishuddi is like a bridge between mind and heart. When it's inactive, we express negative emotions or easily lie, cheat and insult others. We may also feel we are not being heard or we have no voice—we are fearful of speaking up for ourselves. When vishuddi is open it enables clear communication, as well as a flow of energy between mind and heart, or a balance of thought and feeling, giving and receiving, wisdom and compassion. There is a sweetness to our voice and words, and when we speak it is with genuine knowing. Vishuddhi is accessed in the well of the neck in the spinal cord.

6. *Ajna or Third Eye Chakra.* The sixth chakra is the realization of the inner light, that of intuitive understanding and insight, also known as the third eye or wisdom chakra. It is deeply intoxicating, joyful, where great peace resides. The third eye sees the inherent wisdom within rather than looking outward; it sees through limitations to the transcendent wisdom of the awakened mind. Ajna is associated with perception, intuition and insight. The ego was predominant in the solar plexus but here the ego dissolves, as consciousness expands beyond the individual self. But desire is not yet finished and can still pull us back into worldly affairs, as full enlightenment is yet to come.

If ajna is not open then we function from the intellect, which is the greatest obstacle to spiritual development as the intellect likes to think it knows it all. A lack of self-awareness or higher consciousness are examples of an inactive third eye chakra, as are nervous behavior, paranoia or a fear of introspection. This is seen in closed and prejudiced thinking and attitudes, or a resistance to ideas that differ from one's own.

When ajna is open we are able to transcend the intellect, we have the ability to enter into the nature of reality and awaken the truth within. Awakening is not an intellectual pursuit but a balance of head and heart. The wisdom of the awakened mind is connected to the compassion of the heart, just as compassion gives depth to the clarity of insight. One without the other is incomplete: insight without feeling, or compassion without discrimination. Here attachment to matter and form dissolve; there is complete transcendence of duality, of separate self. We awake from the dream, our lives are transformed. Ajna is accessed at the center of the eyebrows looking from within.

7. *Sahasrara or Crown Chakra.* The seventh and highest level of the chakras is where we awaken to full consciousness. This "lotus of the thousand petals" chakra is known as *nirvikalpa samadhi*, or without seed, and is free of samsaras. It is emancipation from the illusive nature of the lower realms and a merging into full realization. Just as waves vanish into the sea, desires and karmas are extinguished; consciousness has expanded to infinity. This is true enlightenment, but it is not so much the end of the journey as the beginning of the real journey, with the emergence of the true and free human.

A closed sahasrara is seen in a strong ego and a resistance to spiritual ideals, which can feel as if life has no meaning. There is emptiness, a vacuum or spiritual void. Conversely, the full surrendering of the ego or the individual self to the radiant divine self is limitless and all embracing. Sahasrara is accessed through the crown of the head.

Through the chakra system we awaken to the depth and innate peace that is deep within the core of our being, our true essence, gaining a deeper appreciation of who we truly are. By bringing awareness to thought patterns, impulses and attitudes we can focus on the different levels of perception as they are manifested in our lives and raise them higher. This is why chakra visualizations are used during Yoga Nidra practice in Chapter 13.

To access a greater understanding of how the chakras affect you, try the following exercise.

TIME-OUT: *Mindful Chakra Awareness*

Find a comfortable place to sit, breathe deeply and relax your body. Close your eyes.

1. Focus your mind on the perineum below the base of your spine and become aware of survival and self-preservation. Let the feelings fill you. Then develop feelings of security and confidence,

knowing that life will unfold as it is meant to
and you will be safe and secure. Breathe and relax.

2. Now focus your mind at the base of the spine and become aware
   of pleasure, desire and pain, of gain and loss, and how the two
   are intertwined. Let the feelings fill you. Then develop feelings of
   confidence, ease and balance, where you are free of basic urges.
   Breathe and relax.

3. Now focus your mind on the navel in the spinal region and
   become aware of the ego, the desire for power and domination.
   Let the feelings fill you. Then develop feelings of inner strength,
   authority and self-assurance. Breathe and relax.

4. Now focus your mind on the heartspace in the depression of the
   chest in the spinal area. Become aware of feeling emotionally
   restricted, cold and selfish. Let the feelings fill you. Then develop
   feelings of open-heartedness, kindness and deep compassion.
   Breathe and relax.

5. Now focus your mind on the well of the neck in the spine. Become
   aware of deceitfulness, cheating and isolation. Let the feelings fill
   you. Then develop feelings of truthfulness, openness and loving
   expression. Breathe and relax.

6. Now focus your mind on the third eye, the wisdom center, at
   the top of the spine. Become aware of feelings of uncertainty,
   unworthiness and mental resistance. Let the feelings fill you. Then
   develop an awareness of seeing the light within to the truth of
   reality. Breathe and relax.

7. Now focus your mind on the crown of your head. Feel a vacuum,
   emptiness and a lack of spiritual awareness. Let the feelings fill
   you. Then experience a complete and joyful surrendering to your
   radiant divine self to the truth beyond understanding. Breathe
   and relax.

Take a few minutes to sit quietly before stretching and opening your eyes.

11

EXPANDING THE MIND

B y now you are probably aware that you are beginning, if you haven't already begun, a journey of self-discovery. Most of us start from a place of finally having reached the limit with too much busy mindedness and chaos, and seek instead a more peaceful life. We begin to realize we don't have to be so pressured and stressed, we absolutely do have choices, and can actually achieve greater joy and peace of mind; we can transform old thinking patterns and habitual ways of being that have limited our happiness. From there the journey to deeper self-understanding unfolds.

As with any journey, we need to make the proper preparations, to have some idea of where we are going and what is needed. What will happen is unique to each one of us for we will each encounter our own particular path and experience our own landscapes. There will undoubtedly be many twists and turns, we may wander off in all sorts of differing directions, at times thinking we have lost sight of the path altogether. But as we develop deeper mindfulness, we gain greater insight, perseverance and a stronger determination to continue.

It may feel as if we are moving from being on automatic pilot to taking control of the ship, or as if we are waking from a long dream.

And in a way, this is exactly what is happening. Just as when we pass through a dark tunnel, there is a moment when it feels endless, we think we might not make it; then suddenly we see the light at the end and the darkness is behind us.

As changes take place it can be tempting to slip back into old ways of being, such as negative thinking or shaming others. Our ego-mind likes to be in charge and convinces us we are not really making progress, that we are not capable of change, or that we really don't have enough time or energy for the journey. But we do. There is always enough time. This is when we have to remind ourselves of our commitment, for we are doing this to gain greater sanity, not to cause more stress.

Every so often it's a good idea to look back at where we were when we started the journey, as it will give us greater strength and encouragement to go on. It's very important to see the progress that has been made and just how far has been traveled, to appreciate the effort and rejoice in the process, rather than feeling hopeless and doubting that any progress is being made at all. Remember a time when you used to get irritated and upset in rush-hour traffic, but now you can sit calmly, breathing and smiling while you wait? That's progress!

We all face difficulties and are constantly challenged, but we don't have to identify with the difficulties. By mindfully relaxing we can relate fully to our everyday existence, yet also be free. A wise teacher once said, "Be in this world but not of it." We can be fully engaged but not become the problem or get lost in the drama. When we respect, honor and trust our inner wisdom we can deal mindfully and calmly with whatever happens.

We are only in this world for a short time, but if we see it as a mystery, an adventure of self-discovery, then we can make the journey a truly magical one. When the innate wisdom that is beyond the rational and intellectual mind is unfolded, we find it isn't an intellectual knowing that will solve life's mysteries, but a deeper knowing that arises from a union of wisdom and compassion.

Being at Peace

We have seen how harming or hurting another is an act of ignorance due to believing there is a separate you and a separate me, rather than knowing we are all interconnected, which means that another person's pain is also our pain. Our enemies are not our enemies; they are simply acting from a limited understanding or ignorance. If someone is at peace they will be unable to harm others, just as no one can harm us if we are peaceful. Peace isn't something that comes and goes, for it is our true nature and is always with us. But just as we can't see our face unless we look in a mirror, it's only when we no longer identify with the me-centered syndrome that we can fully realize the depth of that peace. When we clear away the dust on the mirror we can see our true reflection.

While seeking deeper self-understanding and real peace you may have tried to meditate, but stressful tension prevented you from relaxing enough to enter the quiet. Stress is the physical, mental and emotional obstacle to meditation as it engages the mind in endless distraction and constant chaos. When we want to calm the mind we realize it is filled with more drama than we ever imagined, like a drunken monkey bitten by a scorpion. Of all the things we do probably the most difficult is to just stop and be still! Yet we expect our distracted monkey mind to suddenly become calm and quiet, which results in frustration and boredom. We feel like we are wasting time, so we stop trying. In that way, meditation can actually become another stressful situation.

However, all we need do is learn what precedes meditation and do the groundwork necessary for a successful practice. As a child we begin by crawling, then stand up and fall down many times before we're able to walk. When we are finally sure-footed enough, we can run and dance. It all takes time and practice. The same is true about going within. Before we're ready for meditation, we need to consciously relax. Then, with the mind at peace, meditation will naturally unfold,.

The underlying purpose of Yoga Nidra practice is to release the struggles and stresses that block our ability to go deeper by bringing the clarity of mindful relaxation into every aspect of our lives. This is expressed in our every thought, word and action, a reflection of the peace that is deep within us. Through such knowing our lives are grounded in love and compassion. We realize the many dimensions of consciousness and experience the awakened state more fully.

For thousands of years enlightened yogis and visionaries have explored the vastness of consciousness. They have expounded on the infinite, inexhaustible energy that lies dormant in all beings, and explained that the purpose of life is to find the inner path to self-realization. There are many names given to describe the infinite potential that we are all capable of experiencing, a state that defies the limited pleasure of external existence and reveals the exquisite happiness that can be discovered within us. As we clear away the mud, the brilliance of who we are shines through.

Beneath the superficial layers that obscure our view is a state of serenity, clarity and bliss. It is a natural state, radiating joy and goodness. Just as a diamond is hidden in rough raw stone, there is a priceless jewel waiting to be discovered within us. That is the profundity of life: everything in the world is short-lived and impermanent, but what is innately within us lasts a lifetime. Each action taken with an open heart has the potential to bring us in contact with this precious jewel, and as we move in the direction of its rays we feel its brilliance, luminosity and power. Nothing in life is more satisfying.

A breakthrough happens when we move away from selfish and me-centered behavior toward kindness and compassion for others. This breakthrough may come in a flash or it may be a gentle awakening, our eye of wisdom able to see as if for the first time. When it happens, it feels as familiar as coming home from a long journey. As T. S. Eliot wrote:

> We shall not cease from exploration
> And the end of all our exploring
> Will be to arrive where we started
> And know the place for the first time.

Transformation takes place when change permeates our every cell. Just as a butterfly emerges from its cocoon, so we let go of small-mindedness and merge into the awareness of freedom, of oneness and interconnectedness. We are infinite love and infinite beauty. The realization of truth passes all understanding.

The Next Step

This is the end of Part 1 and understanding the benefits, depth and heart of mindful relaxation. Now it's time to get practical and enter Part 2, the practice of Yoga Nidra. Enjoy!

PART 2

YOGA NIDRA

12

YOGA NIDRA PRACTICALITIES

You are now entering Part 2, which is dedicated to the preparation and practice of Yoga Nidra. This ancient relaxation practice is derived from the yoga teachings originating in India. It literally means sleepless or conscious sleep, a state that looks like sleep but lies between sleep and wakefulness—where we are both awake and deeply relaxed. In yoga this is known as *pratyahara*, or the withdrawal of the mind and senses from the external world.

Throughout the practice you are neither asleep nor distracted by things outside you. All your faculties are functioning, including the intellect, with the focus on the movement of consciousness through the various parts of the body. Consciousness is maintained at a hypnogogic state, the borderline between the conscious and the unconscious mind. Awareness is focused on the movement of the breath as it goes in and out. If your mind drifts, just redirect it to your breathing. By maintaining awareness, you consciously relax the body more deeply than if you were asleep. In this state even self-awareness may dissolve.

There is no need to try to concentrate or follow every instruction; it's more important to maintain an unbroken stream of awareness. If you get overly involved with the words of the practice then the mind will constantly interfere. It doesn't matter if you are thinking throughout the session, or even if you fall asleep. Be patient. You are not relaxing in order to create more stress!

As discussed previously, Yoga Nidra invites a deep level of ease that gives rise to a state of dynamic peace and mindful relaxation with full conscious awareness. It is a means to realizing our deepest aspirations as it cuts through the mental impressions and traumas that are the root of doubts and confusion. Regular practitioners not only find relief from physical and mental stress and tension in the body, but also feel mentally and emotionally balanced and calm.

In this practice you are able to release and move beyond distracting thoughts or impressions and become free of the habitual mind. Both the subconscious and the unconscious mind relax and the impressions that were locked inside can be released. These impressions, or samskaras, are the blocks and obstacles embedded in the deepest parts of your mind that you are unable to consciously recall. For instance, by cutting through the deep mental impressions, the unconscious blocks at the root of doubt, guilt, fear and confusion can be released.

During the process you develop the witness response, which occurs as you watch what is taking place rather than being subjectively involved, enabling you to be free of judgment, overanalysis or rationalization.

On a practical level, Yoga Nidra can be practiced at any time of day. Just don't do it while driving or operating dangerous machinery or equipment!

The Right Place

Before moving on to the instructions in the next chapter, we must create the right environment. Cultivating a supportive atmosphere in which to practice will make a positive difference in your ability to stay focused. You can, of course, practice anywhere, such as on a park bench, by a river or in the bathroom at home, as all you need to do is sit or lie down and close your eyes. Find a place that is quiet and where you will be undisturbed and feel most at ease. Creating a space devoted to this activity—even if it's only a small corner of a room—encourages feelings of self-respect and a reverence for the practice. A specific space will develop its own potency and begin to build in energy.

Remember to turn off the phone and put a note on the door, letting others know when you will be finished. This is exclusively your time and it's important that your nearest and dearest don't resent you for claiming it; so share with them your need to de-stress, which will in turn benefit them. Chances are they will soon be commenting on your improved disposition.

If you practice the short version of Yoga Nidra, detailed in the next chapter, you can do it standing, sitting or lying down. If you practice the longer version, lie down on the floor with a light blanket to cover you and a thin pillow under your head. Wear loose, comfortable clothing so there are no restrictions on your body. Remove your eyeglasses if you wear them, and undo any belts, as this all helps the body be more easeful. If you're lying on your back, have your arms parallel at your sides, a few inches from the body, with your palms facing upward. If you are practicing in order to encourage sleep, then your palms should face downward. Your legs should be slightly apart. Your eyes are closed but you are neither asleep nor fully awake, as the awareness we seek is in the space between sleep and wakefulness. Stay focused as you relax.

Find the best time of day—it may be morning, noon or night, depending on your rhythms and routine. Once you establish a schedule for Yoga Nidra practice, try to stick to it. You will settle more quickly when you practice at a regular time. Respecting your place of practice, as well as a daily time of practice, and knowing that you are creating the opportunity for yourself to relax, will put you in touch with the inspiration and commitment to continue. Soon you will not only look forward to this time, but you also will find it very nourishing and uplifting. It will become such a natural part of your life that you may even wonder how you ever managed without it!

Making Friends with Your Monkey-Mind

When you first begin to practice you will undoubtedly be amazed at how much noise is in your head: the endless thinking, the dramas and scenarios, blame and shame, anxieties, conversations and images that appear never-ending; they seem to go on and on like a monkey leaping from branch to branch. This is very common; it's just that you are rarely quiet enough to notice. Now, for the first time, you are seeking that still place inside, and in the process you experience everything that lies between your busy mind and inner peace.

It is normal to be distracted during the practice; you are not alone in having a noisy monkey mind with a constant stream of thoughts, or a body that keeps coming up with different aches and pains. So don't think that this means you are either unique or hopeless. Although you can't make the mind be quiet, you can stop resisting it by creating the most conducive environment for relaxation to occur.

Every time you notice your mind has drifted off into thinking, you can become the observer, the witness, watching rather than being immersed in the thoughts. It doesn't matter what the thoughts are—all sorts of issues may arise—but just watch and keep coming back to the practice. By being aware of the tendencies of the mind, you will be less disturbed by distractions and less subject to every whim that arises.

Just because your mind goes off in many directions doesn't make you a bad practitioner. By persevering, you will soon get glimpses of that quiet, still place. These glimpses will grow, but it's crucial to be patient with your progress. This is important as it's so easy to judge, whether yourself, your thoughts—or even the technique itself as being wrong or useless.

Boredom is another issue that often arises, particularly if you are used to having a very active mind. It can seem like madness to be spending a whole half hour just being still. Soon you are restless, want to do something or go somewhere. But if you keep practicing, you will eventually be drawn deeper into the quiet.

It's also possible to have a wonderfully peaceful session one day and believe you are really getting somewhere, only to have a boring or noisy practice the next day where you are easily distracted or drift off. This is totally okay! It happens! Don't judge yourself as useless, that's just another way the ego has of distracting you from stillness. Witness how all things come and go, appear and disappear, how nothing stays the same. If you learn to take it all less seriously, the ego-mind won't trouble you so much. Be patient; be gentle. You are a practitioner, not a master. Practice is here to help, not hinder, so make friends with it and enjoy!

The purpose of Yoga Nidra practice is to evoke a state of ease and deep relaxation, insight and realization, to tame the monkey mind and make friends with yourself. Remember, Yoga Nidra is a dynamic relaxation with full conscious awareness, and is a means to realizing your greatest aspirations. It is like looking in a dusty mirror—thoughts and distractions are the dust, and you think you are the distorted image. But beneath the dust is your true image, just as beneath the thoughts and confusions is the radiance of your true being.

Stages of Practice

Yoga Nidra has distinct stages that progressively deepen the relaxation. Rotation of consciousness, visualizations and images are used to focus attention and enhance awareness, while a resolve is used to create a positive affirmation and deeper purpose.

In the longer version of Yoga Nidra you will start by rotating awareness through the various parts of the body. Using electrode stimuli, scientific researchers have shown that each part of the body is directly connected to a specific part of the brain that also deals with feelings, sensations and thought patterns. Awareness of each part of the body is through a rotation of consciousness in a similar sequence to the body being mapped in the brain. It is based on the yogic system of *nyasa*, literally meaning "to take the mind to that point."

By rotating consciousness in this way, from one part of the body to the next, you connect body, brain, emotions and mental awareness into a unified whole. As you become familiar with this particular sequence of relaxation you can "tune in" at any time, whether during the practice or not.

Further on in the practice you pay attention to the opposites: sensations of heaviness and lightness, or hot and cold. This works directly with the parts of the brain responsible for balancing your inner and outer environment, and your sensual experience. It harmonizes and eases the two-way communication between experience and response to stimuli.

For instance, as you become aware of the initial feeling of heaviness it sends a message to the brain to let go and "sink into the ground." In this way the muscles and tendons are eased. As you reach this state, you are then directed to develop the experience of lightness, as if floating. This relaxes the body more and also begins to separate consciousness from the physical experience.

Then you focus on the opposite experiences of hot or cold. These two conditions are related to your emotions: you become hot with anger and passion, or cold with hate and rage. By experiencing the opposites in a deeply relaxed state, you begin to release the feelings that are beyond your conscious reach.

Or you may focus on the space between the body and the floor, bringing awareness to the slightest contact so that the mind is fully focused.

Sankalpa *or Resolve*

At both the beginning and end of the practice, when the mind is in a state of dynamic relaxation, you will repeat a resolve or affirmation, known as a *sankalpa*, which is what makes Yoga Nidra different and more powerful than other forms of relaxation. Whatever you put into the mind while it is uncluttered, clear and free of distractions, will take root. By making your sankalpa while relaxed, you are opening to deeper transformation.

The resolve is an affirmation of what you know you want to achieve at this stage or during your lifetime. Each one of us needs to find the resolve that is meaningful for us. Let it be realistic and simple. There's no need to work on more than one issue at a time, rather focus on your main priority. It should consist of a positive statement, such as "I am fully relaxed and capable" or "I am strong and fearless." It should also be brief so it is easy to remember. You can repeat it as often as you like, in or out of the practice. Keep it to yourself, as it will become stronger if it remains private. Some examples are as follows:

I am an instrument of unconditional love

With every breath I am more at peace

I am at one with my true nature

Loving-kindness and compassion fill my heart

I am deepening in my awareness of unconditional happiness

Each time you practice Yoga Nidra you will repeat the same resolve so that it takes root in the unconscious mind. This is why it is important that the resolve be one you feel deeply. Just as the old impressions may influence your behavior in a dysfunctional way, so the resolve can influence your behavior and actions to bring about transformation.

A resolve is a means to create a whole new positive direction in life and its power can't be underestimated. However, you may need to clear external obstacles—like drug or alcohol abuse—before such transformation can fully manifest itself. If necessary, use the resolve for therapeutic reasons so that behavior patterns like these can change, even though a resolve is not specifically about giving up smoking or losing weight; rather it is a statement of intent reflecting your truer aspiration. Always remember the resolve is about what is most meaningful in the whole of your life.

The resolve helps unfold your potential and higher objectives. With one-pointed awareness it gathers the scattered energies of the mind to focus on what is important for you. When the resolve is planted in the relaxed mind, then the very nature of its power clears away whatever is preventing its successful fruition. It is a way of taking action to make a difference, rather than staying stuck in old ways of self-pity, despair or helplessness.

A resolve is a declaration of a positive desire, and through it you will find strength and guidance; putting it into action gives your life deeper meaning and a new forward-looking direction. It's a way to release whatever is limiting you. The resolve becomes the foundation from which you grow, a seed that facilitates positive motivation. The mind is a perfect instrument, and a good practitioner can play very beautiful music with it.

Visualization

In a later stage, visualizations are developed as a means of connecting with the impressions buried in the unconscious; old impressions are replaced with healing and caring images, creating a profound sense of well-being and inner joy. If it's hard to visualize, then see the image as a thought. It's not necessary to try too hard since this is not a concentration practice—just be focused and aware. As you go deeper in your practice and focus your mind, so the images will come more easily and clearly.

Yoga Nidra enables you to make the connection between the unconscious and the waking state, so you develop a deeper sense of communication within yourself. Rather than being in a passive or forgetful state, as after sleeping or dreaming, you are fully awake so the imagery can enter the conscious mind. As the conscious and the unconscious come together, you will have access to a vast amount of information. This new, broader landscape should impart a new sense of freedom.

Closing

When you are finished, make sure you have time to gradually emerge from the deep Yoga Nidra state. Fully externalize your mind and all the senses of the body before moving on with the rest of your day. The more you practice the more quickly you will awaken to the brilliance of Yoga Nidra.

13

YOGA NIDRA PRACTICE

This chapter includes three practices: a short Yoga Nidra that takes five to ten minutes and can be done anywhere in a quiet place, whether standing, sitting, or lying down; a long Yoga Nidra and Yoga Nidra: Awakening the Chakras, both of which take twenty to thirty minutes and are done lying down.

Short Yoga Nidra

Wear loose, comfortable clothing. Arms are by your side or resting on your knees, palms facing upward and eyes are closed. Take a deep breath and let it out.

Relax your body by bringing awareness to your feet and working your way upward, releasing tension wherever it may linger . . . in the feet . . . ankles . . . calves . . . knees . . . thighs . . . buttocks . . . spine . . . shoulder blades . . . pelvis . . . stomach . . . chest . . . hands . . . wrists . . . lower arms . . . elbows . . . upper arms . . . shoulders . . . neck . . . head.

Watch the incoming and outgoing breath, breathing naturally, for a few moments. Silently repeat three times to yourself, "I am aware I am practicing Yoga Nidra." Stay awake, and if the mind drifts bring it back to the practice.

Now create a resolve, a positive affirmation concerning something meaningful you know you want to achieve. Resolves made in life may or may not come true, but the resolve made at the beginning and end of Yoga Nidra will come true. Repeat the resolve three times to yourself.

Now visualize a red rose in the center of your chest in the region of your heart—the heartspace—a beautiful red rose with many petals. Feel the soft texture, see the color, smell the fragrance. Stay with this image for a few moments.

Feel your heart opening like the petals of the rose. The feeling of unconditional love fills your heart. This love is universal happiness, divine love that nourishes you from within. Feel peace and joy emanating. Breathe into your heart. With each breath feel your love expanding and embracing all beings.

Peace, peace, peace. Repeat the resolve that you made at the beginning of the practice. Repeat three times. Become aware of your breath as it enters and leaves your body. Stay with this for a few moments. The practice of Yoga Nidra is over.

Externalize your awareness. Become aware of your breathing, your feet, legs, arms, trunk, shoulders and head. Move the body gently and become aware of the room you are in. Take a few breaths, then open your eyes and have a smile on your face.

Long Yoga Nidra: Inner Conscious Relaxation

This practice is done lying down. Wear loose, comfortable clothing, have a light blanket to cover you. Find a comfortable posture on a mat or blanket and use a small pillow beneath your head. Arms are parallel to your body, palms upward, legs are slightly apart and eyes are closed. Take a deep breath and let it out.

Part One: Rotation

Relax your body by bringing awareness to your feet and working your way upward, releasing tension wherever it may linger . . . in the feet . . .

ankles . . . calves . . . knees . . . thighs . . . buttocks . . . spine . . . shoulder blades . . . pelvis . . . stomach . . . chest . . . hands . . . wrists . . . lower arms . . . elbows . . . upper arms . . . shoulders . . . neck . . . head.

Watch the incoming and outgoing breath, breathing naturally, for a few moments. Silently repeat three times to yourself, "I am aware I am practicing Yoga Nidra." Stay awake and if the mind drifts, bring it back to the practice.

Become aware of the breath, as it enters and leaves the body. The breath enters both nostrils, like a triangle with no base, then exhale. Feel you are seated in the nostrils. Do this for a few moments.

Now create a resolve, a positive affirmation concerning something meaningful you know you want to achieve. The resolve is a simple sentence with little punctuation. Resolves made in life may or may not come true, but the resolve made at the beginning and end of Yoga Nidra will come true. Repeat the resolve three times to yourself.

Next is the rotation of consciousness. Visualize a part of the physical body, and repeat that part in your mind. If it is easy, fine, and if not just stay with the practice.

Starting with the right thumb . . . second finger . . . third finger . . . fourth finger . . . fifth finger . . . palm of the right hand . . . back of the hand . . . right wrist . . . lower arm . . . elbow . . . upper arm . . . right shoulder . . . armpit . . . right side of the waist . . . hip . . . thigh . . . knee . . . calf . . . ankle . . . heel . . . sole of the right foot . . . ball of the right foot . . . big toe . . . second toe . . . third toe . . . fourth toe . . . fifth toe.

Become aware of the left thumb . . . second finger . . . third finger . . . fourth finger . . . fifth finger . . . palm of the left hand . . . back of the hand . . . left wrist . . . lower arm . . . elbow . . . upper arm . . . left shoulder . . . armpit . . . left side of the waist . . . hip . . . thigh . . . knee . . . calf . . . ankle . . . heel . . . sole of the left foot . . . ball of the left foot . . . big toe . . . second toe . . . third toe . . . fourth toe . . . fifth toe.

Now become aware of the right shoulder blade . . . left shoulder blade . . . spinal cord . . . right buttock . . . left buttock . . . and the whole of the back together.

Awareness of the genitals . . . pelvis . . . belly . . . navel . . . abdomen . . . right side of the chest . . . left side of the chest . . . hollow of the chest . . .

well of the neck . . . neck . . . chin . . . upper lip . . . lower lip . . . both lips together . . . right cheek . . . left cheek . . . nose . . . nose tip . . . right ear . . . left ear . . . right temple . . . left temple . . . right eye . . . left eye . . . right eyelid . . . left eyelid . . . right eyebrow . . . left eyebrow . . . center of the eyebrows . . . forehead . . . top of the head . . . whole body . . . whole body . . . whole body. Repeat to yourself, "I am aware of the whole of my physical body."

Part Two: The Opposites

The next phase of Yoga Nidra is being aware of the opposites, starting with the feeling of heaviness. Create the feeling of heaviness in your body . . . your legs are heavy . . . your buttocks . . . back . . . arms . . . chest . . . head . . . your whole body is feeling heavy . . . as if you are sinking into the ground . . . stay with this for a few moments. Now create the feeling of lightness . . . bring lightness to the body . . . to your fingers . . . arms . . . stomach . . . chest . . . back . . . legs . . . shoulders . . . neck . . . your whole body is light . . . as if you are floating on a cloud . . . stay with this for a few moments.

Now create the feeling of coldness . . . in your body . . . your hands . . . feet . . . buttocks . . . feel a chill up your spine . . . your whole body is getting colder . . . you are walking in the snow. . . stay with this for a few moments. Now create the feeling of heat . . . in your hands . . . in your right foot . . . left foot. . . . stomach . . . chest . . . lips . . . in the whole of your body . . . you are walking in the desert . . . the noonday sun is above . . . feel the heat as if you are sweating . . . stay with this for a few moments.

Part Three: Visualization

Visualize you are walking down a country lane. The air is laden with the scent of wildflowers, the sun is warming your back, the birds are singing. You come to a small path leading across the fields, and carefree as a child, you play there amongst the flowers. The path leads you on to an old wood filled with beautiful trees, animals playing in the shade. You feel safe and welcomed here. In the center of the wood is a glade filled with streaming sunlight. As you walk toward this glade, with each step you feel renewed and revitalized. As you enter the glade you feel you are entering a special and sacred place.

From the far side of the glade you see a figure coming toward you: a holy woman, a gentle, loving being. You sit together in the glade. You feel a healing power and purity flowing through you. The holy woman offers you words of wisdom. You feel deep gratitude in your heart.

Part Four: Ending

Peace, peace, peace. Repeat the resolve that you made at the beginning of Yoga Nidra three times. The practice of Yoga Nidra is over. Become aware of your breath, as it enters and leaves the body. Stay with this for a few moments.

Become aware of your feet, legs, arms, trunk, shoulders and head. Move the body gently and become aware of the room you are in. Take your time, and make sure you are externalized. Roll on your side, take a few breaths, then sit up, open your eyes and have a smile on your face.

Yoga Nidra: Awakening the Chakras

This practice is done lying down. Wear loose, comfortable clothing, have a light blanket to cover you. Find a comfortable posture on a mat or blanket and use a small pillow beneath your head. Arms are parallel to your body, palms upward, legs are slightly apart and eyes are closed. Take a deep breath and let it out.

Part One: Rotation

Relax your body by bringing awareness to your feet and working your way upward, releasing tension wherever it may linger . . . in the feet . . . ankles . . . calves . . . knees . . . thighs . . . buttocks . . . spine. . . shoulder blades . . . pelvis . . . stomach . . . chest . . . hands . . . wrists . . . lower arms . . . elbows . . . upper arms . . . shoulders . . . neck . . . head.

Watch the incoming and outgoing breath, breathing naturally, for a few moments. Silently repeat three times to yourself, "I am aware I am practicing Yoga Nidra." Stay awake and if the mind drifts, bring it back to the practice.

Become aware of the breath, as it enters and leaves the body. The breath enters both nostrils, like a triangle with no base, then exhale. Feel you are seated in the nostrils. Do this for a few minutes.

Now create a resolve, a positive affirmation concerning something meaningful you know you want to achieve. Resolves made in life may or may not come true, but the resolve made at the beginning and end of Yoga Nidra will come true. Repeat the resolve three times to yourself. The resolve is a simple sentence with little punctuation.

Next is the rotation of consciousness. Visualize a part of the physical body, and repeat that part in your mind. If it is easy, fine, and if not just stay with the practice.

Starting with right thumb . . . second finger . . . third finger . . . fourth finger . . . fifth finger . . . palm of the right hand . . . back of the hand . . . right wrist . . . lower arm . . . elbow . . . upper arm . . . right shoulder . . . armpit . . . right side of the waist . . . hip . . . thigh . . . knee . . . calf . . . ankle . . . heel . . . sole of the right foot . . . ball of the right foot . . . big toe . . . second toe . . . third toe . . . fourth toe. . . fifth toe.

Become aware of the left thumb . . . second finger . . . third finger . . . fourth finger . . . fifth finger . . . palm of the left hand . . . back of the hand . . . left wrist . . . lower arm . . . elbow . . . upper arm . . . left shoulder . . . armpit . . . left side of the waist . . . hip . . . thigh . . . knee . . . calf . . . ankle . . . heel . . . sole of the left foot . . . ball of the left foot . . . big toe . . . second toe . . . third toe . . . fourth toe . . . fifth toe.

Now become aware of the right shoulder blade . . . left shoulder blade . . . spinal cord . . . right buttock . . . left buttock . . . and the whole of the back together.

Awareness of the genitals . . . pelvis . . . belly . . . navel . . . abdomen . . . right side of the chest . . . left side of the chest . . . hollow of the chest . . . well of the neck . . . neck . . . chin . . . upper lip . . . lower lip . . . both lips together . . . right cheek . . . left cheek. . . nose . . . nose tip . . . right ear . . .

left ear. . . right temple . . . left temple . . . right eye . . . left eye . . . right eyelid . . . left eyelid . . . right eyebrow . . . left eyebrow . . . center of the eyebrows . . . forehead . . . top of the head . . . whole body . . . whole body . . . whole body. Repeat to yourself, "I am aware of the whole of my physical body."

Part Two: The Gap

Now become aware of the contact between your physical body and the ground beneath you . . . bring attention to wherever your body meets the ground, beginning with your right leg and the ground . . . be aware of the point of contact and focus your attention on that space . . . the point of contact between your left leg and the ground . . . stay with your awareness there for a few moments ... of your right arm and the ground . . . awareness of that space . . . of your left arm and the ground . . . attention on that space. Now your buttocks and the ground . . . awareness of the meeting point and the space . . . your back and the ground . . . stay with this for a few moments. Now the meeting point between your head and the ground . . . of the whole of your physical body and the ground . . . get closer to the awareness of this space.

Now let your mind scan your body and become aware of any sensations: pleasant or unpleasant, pleasurable or not pleasurable. Breathe into this. Continue to scan your body, going from one part to another, simply observing. Stay with this for a few moments.

Part Three: Chakra Visualization

The chakras, or levels of consciousness, are not physical but they can be accessed at certain points in the spinal region. Start at the base and move upward. Take your mind to where they are located, visualize the symbol and repeat the name.

Muladhara, the first chakra, is located at the perineum. It is represented by a deep red lotus flower with four petals; within it is a symbol, a red inverted triangle with a pink serpent with three and a half coils, its head looking downward, the fangs protruding from its mouth. Take your mind to that area. Silently repeat three times "Muladhara, muladhara, muladhara" as you visualize the image.

Swadhisthana, the second chakra, is located at the base of the spine in the coccyx. It is an orange-red lotus flower with six petals. The symbol represents unconsciousness, depicted as an endless sea in the dark night. Take your mind to that point, at the base of the spine. Silently repeat three times "Swadhisthana, swadhisthana, swadhisthana" as you visualize this image.

Manipura, the third chakra, is located in the spinal cord at the level of the navel. Take your mind to that point, at the level of the navel in the spinal cord. It is represented by a bright yellow lotus with ten petals, and within it is a yellow sunflower with a red inverted triangle. Silently repeat three times "Manipura, manipura, manipura" as you visualize this image.

Anahata, the fourth chakra, is located at the impression of the chest in the spinal cord. It is symbolized by a blue lotus flower with twelve petals, and within it is the symbol of a small candle flame. Take your mind to that point at the hollow of the chest in the spinal cord. Repeat mentally three times "Anahata, anahata, anahata," and visualize the small flame of a candle.

Vishuddhi, the fifth chakra, is located at the well of the neck in the spinal cord. It is represented by a purple lotus flower with sixteen petals, and within it are nectar drops and the feeling of coolness. Take your mind to that point, at the well of the neck in the spinal cord. Repeat mentally three times "Vishuddhi, vishuddhi, vishuddhi," and visualize this image.

Ajna, the sixth chakra, is located at the level of the center of the eyebrows, looking from within. It is represented by a translucent gray/silver lotus flower with two petals, with the symbol of the third eye. There is a feeling of intoxication, as if drunk with bliss, and this is where you first see the light of truth and wisdom. Take your mind to the point between the eyebrows from the inside. Repeat mentally three times "Ajna, ajna, ajna," and feel the great bliss of intoxication.

Sahasrara, the seventh chakra, is situated at the crown of the head, about an inch inside. It is represented by a thousand-petaled, bright red lotus flower. One petal is much bigger than your head, much bigger than many heads. Take your mind to the crown of the head one inch inside. Repeat mentally three times "Sahasrara, sahasrara, sahasrara," and visualize one petal of the thousand-petaled lotus.

Now rotate awareness through the chakras, touching each center with your mind, trying to visualize the symbol while going up and down the spine. If it is difficult to visualize the symbol, just bring your mind to the chakra center mentally; repeat the name and move on to the next one, going up and down, touching each center with the mind.

Muladhara perineum, swadhisthana base of the spine, manipura navel center, anahata hollow of the chest, vishuddhi well of the neck, ajna center of the eyebrows from the inside, sahasrara crown of the head from the inside. Now downward: sahasrara, ajna, vishuddhi, anahata, manipura, swadhisthana, muladhara.

Repeat once again, going up and down the energy centers a little faster: muladhara, swadhisthana, manipura, anahata, vishuddhi, ajna, sahasrara; sahasrara, ajna, vishuddhi, anahata, manipura, swadhisthana, muladhara.

Now go to the center of the brain. Focus your awareness on the tiny white light you find there. As you visualize the white light notice it gets bigger and bigger. Stay with this for a few moments.

Part Four: Ending

Peace, peace, peace. Repeat the resolve that you made at the beginning of Yoga Nidra three times. The practice of Yoga Nidra is over. Become aware of your breath, as it enters and leaves the body. Stay with this for a few moments.

Become aware of your feet, legs, arms, trunk, shoulders and head. Move the body gently and become aware of the room you are in. Take your time, and make sure you are externalized. Roll on your side, take a few breaths, then sit up, open your eyes and have a smile on your face.

ABOUT THE AUTHOR

Ed Shapiro was born in the Bronx, New York, became a New York City dance champion, a yogi, skier, skydiver, and bungee jumper. Deb, from the English countryside, is the granddaughter of Sir Winston Churchill's editor. While Ed trained in Yoga Nidra in India, where he became Swami Brahmananda, a Yoga Master, Deb was training in meditation in London and is a respected Bodymind expert.

Ed and Deb both began meditating in the late 1960s, studying with such respected Yoga and Buddhist teachers as the Dalai Lama, Woodstock guru Swami Satchidananda, Tai Situ Rinpoche, and crazy wisdom Buddhist teacher Chogyam Trungpa Rinpoche. They have been teaching together for thirty years, leading mindful relaxation and meditation retreats worldwide; they had their own TV show in London, *Chill Out*, and an international radio show, *Going out of Your Mind*. The Shapiros are corporate consultants and personal coaches working with CEOs and senior management.

Ed and Deb are the authors of many books on relaxation, meditation, personal development, and the bodymind relationship, published in over twenty languages. Contributors to their books include the Dalai Lama, Paul McCartney, President Gorbachev, Richard Gere, Marianne

Williamson, Yoko Ono, Jon Kabat-Zinn, and Jane Fonda. They are bloggers for Awaken.com, Care2.com, Oprah.com, ThriveGlobal.com, HuffPost.com, and others.

Their books include *The Unexpected Power of Mindfulness & Meditation* and *Your Body Speaks Your Mind: Decoding the Emotional, Physical, and Spiritual Messages That Underlie Illness* (winner of the Visionary Book Award in Alternative Health). Both longer Yoga Nidra practices are available to download, and a CD is available on request. For more information, see www.EdandDebShapiro.com.